Spokane Conference 3/31/74
Sister Mary T. Buttemer, O.P.

Gifts of the Spirit and the Body of Christ

Gifts of the Spirit and the Body of Christ

PERSPECTIVES ON THE CHARISMATIC MOVEMENT

EDITED BY
J. ELMO AGRIMSON

AUGSBURG PUBLISHING HOUSE
MINNEAPOLIS, MINNESOTA

GIFTS OF THE SPIRIT AND THE BODY OF CHRIST

Library of Congress Catalog Card No. 73-88608

International Standard Book No. 0-8066-1411-0

Manufactured in the United States of America

Contents

Preface

J. Elmo Agrimson
President
Southeastern Minnesota District
The American Lutheran Church
St. Paul, Minnesota

Preface

"The wind blows where it wills, and you hear the sound of it, but you do not know whence it comes or whither is goes; so it is with every one who is born of the Spirit" (John 3:8).

Moods and movements of varying intensity are flowing through religious life in America. The fifties brought crowds of people into American churches. Following this period of popular religiosity came a few convulsive years of social protest, prophetic judgment of individual and corporate indifference, racism, poverty, Vietnam. Even the church as an institution was indicted for her muscle-bound bureaucratic traditions. Although the conscience of America had been pricked, a gradually sickening despair has followed the frustrated idealistic expectations of our national and international goals.

Recently the American mood has receded inwardly. Apathy, despair, loneliness, alienation, loss of identity have displaced a zest and a faith in "progress." Instead of a theological frame of reference for our faith we seem to be seeking a holy grail of warm and intense intimacy. Much of our religious life thus has become more individualistic, subjective, apocalyptic, and simplistic. In some groups the traditional supports and guides for the Christian life—the Bible, doctrine, biblical history, liturgy—have been eclipsed by an exotic cloud of experiential ecstasy. This runs parallel to our current political and social pattern of the last five years. We have assumed an anti-intellectual and apathetic attitude to the solution of life situations. We want less discipline from traditional theological search, biblical prophetic critique, and objective examination of life style, ethics, and devotional expression.

In the midst of this mood or trend in American religious life comes the charismatic movement, sometimes called neo-pentecostalism. The phenomenon is often found in such traditional groupings as the Catholic, Episcopal, and Lutheran churches. This book is an attempt to gather a few observations from several persons in the Lutheran church who have reflected on the phenomenon. Changes and trends in religious life, especially as they affect The American Lutheran Church, are the concern of this book. One of the writers is in the Lutheran charismatic movement.

The charismatic movement is a new lay assertion of different proportions in the church. Discovery that the *gifts* of the spirit belong to the congregation, not to an ecclesiastically controlled dispensation system, has influenced people who have previously been unresponsive to speak and act in the church. It seems to have encouraged a self assertion and zeal among the faithful that has been lacking before. God's movement among us can not be wholly defined or traditionally regulated by church organization whether it be the local pastor, district, or national church administration. This may have a lot to do with the intense outflow of personal feeling and sense of freedom in the new informal groups. This possibly explains why the charismatic movement moves easily across denominational lines. One gets the impression that the old wineskin can not hold us and authority can not control us. However, it is obvious that new authority figures and new definitions soon appear in the group itself.

Much of the material in this book is supported by my observations in meeting with congregations and individuals who have had a recent charismatic or pentecostal exposure. These kinds of resources have assisted me when meeting with pastors, congregational leaders, and congregations in assembly. They helped provide a climate of understanding, openness, respect, and unity as a Christian group. Therefore, the book is intended mainly to be of help to pastors and congregational leaders. The effort reflects concern for the health of the church, the body of Christ.

The proper use of *gifts,* speaking in tongues, prophesying, administration, pastoral care, has been a matter of concern, a matter needing guidance, a matter often calling for rigid discipline in the struggle for order in the history of the church. In conversing with congregations upset over the charismatic appearance in their midst, I often warn them against making this issue the center of a power struggle in the church. People easily choose up sides. A power struggle may become the most ecstatic option to break the boredom in any institution, in the church, in the government, or in the family. Our hope is that this book might assist a few people to better understand the richness of the Christian community, the deep spiritual springs of the church, the great quality we can give to the body of Christ—the spirit of *love* and *unity.*

This book might seem too matter of fact and descriptive. Religious experience belongs to the center of human thoughts and feelings and should be respected as such. It is one thing to describe people's actions. It is quite another to research the meaning of their deep personal mysteries. However, the pentecostals place great emphasis on evidence of experience. The writers in this book have given us their perspective from several points of view. This may be helpful to give us an understanding of a more subjective religious activity in our time. I hope we can keep a good balance between respect for individual religious experience and a wholesome unity in the congregation. Each chapter has a specific framework—biblical, historical, sociological, psychological, and practical.

The New Testament references to "gift" (*charis,* i.e. charismatic) are given detailed treatment by Dr. Duane Priebe. This chapter may seem academic. However, unless we examine the scriptures thoroughly for background on such movements our religious claims would flow like emotional floodwaters, drowning the greater gifts of love, patience, kindness, justice, and peace. Although it is occasionally good to have feelings of love and enthusiasm overflow the traditional patterns of church life, the source of the Christian faith and life comes from the word and person of Jesus Christ translated into human lives by the inner activity of the Holy Spirit.

Professor Paul Sonnack, in his chapter describing the

history of revival movements in America, should assist us in understanding our present day religious expression. One could, of course, go back to the time of the Montanists in the second century who emphasized ecstatic utterances, end-time prophecies, the second coming of Jesus, and no second marriages. However, Mr. Sonnack gives an excellent background for revivalism in America, whose course was definitely set by Charles G. Finney. One can not understand the religious life of our country unless he has looked at a few threads of church history which weave through our past and up to the present moment on the American scene.

Dr. Johannes Schiller indicates how the events in history, especially the change in familiar patterns of community stability, influence our religious outlook. I am personally convinced from my own observations, a little study, and occasional confrontation, that the depersonalization, loneliness, and sense of powerlessness among many people today has much to do with new trends in the life of the church. The church itself may at times seem formal, unfeeling, dull in its preaching and liturgy. Little opportunity may be given for personal contact either in times of joy or haunting despair. Therefore, we must seriously consider what Dr. Schiller is talking about.

The psychological dimension of religious experience receives interesting analysis from Dr. Kildahl. Although there resides a serious danger in psychological assessment of religion, many intense human feelings of religious nature benefit from objective examination. The hazard comes when we try to explain away the reality of any human feeling. Religion can feed on neurotic pulsation, but it can also be a free response to the gospel of forgiveness, love, and hope. The charismatic movement is associated with considerable intense feeling in our traditional patterns of church life.

From the charismatic movement in Germany, Dr. Arnold Bittlinger writes a profound chapter on baptism and the Holy Spirit. This issue has most often been the source of dissension and difficulty in congregations. Christians should evaluate their new experiences and their need to express themselves in the context of the community of the believers. This chapter should have special meaning for those who are in the movement.

This book does not represent an official position of The American Lutheran Church, nor do the authors of the different chapters necessarily agree. The concluding chapter reflects my experiences in trying to assist congregations which have experienced a neo-pentecostal emphasis to understand, benefit from, and guide this movement.

I am indebted to many people in the charismatic movement and also to many others not in the movement for insight and encouragement in the attempt to build up the Body of Christ.

1

Charismatic Gifts and Christian Existence in Paul

Duane A. Priebe
Asst. Professor of Theology
Wartburg Theological Seminary
Dubuque, Iowa

1

Charismatic Gifts and Christian Existence in Paul

In ordinary usage, the word *charisma* refers to a person with special leadership ability or an exceptional degree of personal magnetism. Hence, a charismatic figure often appears to be elevated above the level of ordinary men. We also use the word in a religious context when we speak of the charismatic movement. In this sense, it often connotes participation in extraordinary phenomena—speaking in tongues, ecstatic prophecy, miraculous powers, faith healing—which are understood as manifestations of the power of the Holy Spirit at work in human existence. There is also a tendency to set those who have experienced charismatic manifestations, such as speaking in tongues, apart from other people as those who have been filled with the Holy Spirit.

References to Charismatic Gifts in Acts

In the New Testament there are only a limited number of passages that make explicit reference to such extraordinary manifestations as a part of Christian existence. Apart from Paul's letters to the church at Corinth (esp. 1 Cor. 12-14 and 2 Cor. 10-13) the primary material is in the book of Acts,[1] where the mission of the apostles and Paul is often accompanied by healings and other miracles. This appears to be a characteristic emphasis of Luke, although similar manifestations are mentioned elsewhere in the New Testament (e.g. in the mission of the Twelve in Mark 6:13; also Gal. 3:5). Speaking in tongues is used in Acts to accent certain points within the overall structure of the book.

In Acts 2:1ff. speaking in tongues is not described as the incoherent speech mentioned elsewhere, but it is a miracle of communication enabling the people gathered around to hear the mighty works of God proclaimed in their own languages.[2] As such it expresses the work of the Holy Spirit in overcoming the barriers that separate men from one another. At the same time it serves to identify the Christian community as the eschatological people of God, i.e., as the community in which the end of history and the fulfillment of all God's promises has become an actuality in the outpouring of the Spirit (vv. 14ff.).

The story in Acts 19:1-7 in which Paul meets people who had only been baptized with John's baptism (apparently disciples of the Baptist) serves to stress the difference between John's baptism and Christian baptism. Only Jesus' work is the ground of the giving of the Spirit, and only the Christian community is the eschatological community of the Spirit.

In the story of the conversion of Cornelius in Acts 10 (esp. vv. 44-48) the phenomena of speaking in tongues and prophecy drive the Christian mission beyond the boundaries of Judaism and authenticate the Gentile mission.

In Acts 8:14ff., after the initial success of Philip in Samaria, the reception of the Spirit is accompanied by some unspecified overt manifestation. Here it serves to accent the authority of the twelve apostles (a characteristic theme in Acts) over the life and development of the early church.

In all cases, speaking in tongues is not itself the matter of interest, but it is one of the ingredients that characterize the early Christian community. A second point to be noted is that Acts clearly presupposes that *all Christians have received the fullness of the Spirit.*[3] A third is that the gift of the Spirit is not identified with extraordinary manifestations, although it is clear that Luke seems to presuppose that there will be such manifestations within the community of the Spirit.

Spiritual enthusiasm and extraordinary manifestations of the Spirit probably were significant features of the life of the early Christian community.[4] Among other things, this reflected a desire of people in that day to participate in transcendent power. This desire found many forms of religious expression in the first century world. Within this setting, the early church was a community that was caught up into the rule of the exalted Lord Jesus Christ, and his power was present among them. In the Holy Spirit a person already participated in the new life of the new age of God's rule, which had become a reality in Jesus' resurrection (cf. Eph. 2:4-7; Col. 3:12-13). Christian existence was surrounded by the glory of the crucified, resurrected, and exalted Lord, whose rule extends to the entire universe (Eph. 1:19-23; Col. 1:11-20). For reflection on the role of such manifestations of the Spirit in the life of the Christian community and the problems it can pose, it is necessary to consider Paul's discussions in 1 and 2 Corinthians.

What the Word Means

Charisma (plural *charismata*) is a Greek word meaning "favor" or "divine gift." It is closely related to *charis,* which is the word translated "grace" in the New Testament. Apart from 1 Peter 4:10, the word *charisma* is only used in the Pauline literature, where it can be used in a variety of related ways. In Romans 5:15, 16; 6:23 *charisma* refers to the gracious gift of righteousness or salvation given us through Jesus Christ. As such it is used interchangeably with the Greek word for "gift," and is translated "free gift" in the RSV. Similarly, Romans 11:29 uses the plural *charismata* with reference to God's election of Israel as his people, which makes them beloved of God, for his gifts and call are irrevocable. Thus in these passages *charisma* refers to the event in which God bestows salvation or righteousness on men or elects them to be his people. It accents the character of this event as his gracious gift. In Romans 1:11 and 2 Corinthians 1:11 the word refers to a benefit or favor of an unspecified sort that is granted a person. In the former, Paul speaks of his imparting some *charisma* to the Roman congregation which will strengthen them, and then he qualifies this by speaking about being mutually encouraged by one another's faith. In the latter the *charisma* is given to Paul and his associates by God in answer to prayers on their behalf.

The word *charisma* is used of gifts of the Spirit in the

sense of special capacities or powers (Rom. 12:6; 1 Cor. 1:7; 7:7; 12:4, 9, 28, 30, 31; 1 Tim. 4:14; 2 Tim. 1:6; 1 Pet. 4:10). 1 Corinthians 1:7, where Paul thanks God that they do not lack any *charisma,* is related to the later discussion in chapters 12-14. 1 Corinthians 7:7 involves a specific *charisma,* namely the gift of celibacy. However, Paul emphasizes that different people receive different gifts.[5] The letters to Timothy, which are later in the first century and reflect the movement toward a more structured, institutional form of the church, speak of a *charisma* which Timothy has been given by prophecy (1 Tim. 4:14) and by laying on of hands (1 Tim. 4:14; 2 Tim. 1:6). In 1 Timothy 4:14 the reference appears to be to the pastoral office and its duties, which include the public reading of Scripture, preaching, and teaching. Timothy is urged to make progress in the performance of these duties through practice. In 2 Timothy 1:6 reference is made to his faith together with power, love, and self-control. In 1 Corinthians 12:9, 28, 30 the plural *charismata* is used in the phrase "gifts of healing," which is apparently a fixed expression.

Romans 12, 1 Corinthians 12, and 1 Peter 4 include lists of the *charismata.* When we compare these lists,[6] the similarities and differences in character of the items included in the lists is striking. Extraordinary manifestations of the Spirit characterize the lists in 1 Corinthians 12-14. All the lists include tongues, prophecy,[7] working miracles, and gifts of healing (the latter two probably being included in the concept of faith that moves mountains in 13:2), while the closely related gift of interpreting tongues is mentioned in two of the lists. Outside of 1 Corinthians, the lists of *charismata* are not characterized by extraordinary manifestations of the Spirit, but by special capacities for helping others in the community. The list in Ephesians 4 seems to refer to offices in the organizational structure of the church as it was developing. Of the items common to the lists in 1 Corinthians, only prophecy occurs in these other lists. If there were any common core around which such lists were built, it would seems to be apostles, prophecy, and teaching. But the content of the lists can vary considerably, and the precise character of the gifts of the Spirit included is probably related to the forms the manifestations of the Spirit took in a particular Christian community. This would suggest that while manifestations of the Spirit such as tongues, working miracles, and gifts of healing characterized the Corinthian community, this was not necessarily the case in other Christian communities, even though such manifestations occurred elsewhere. Nor do they seem to be the characteristic manifestations of the Spirit, for the most characteristic gifts seem to be those most closely associated with love and which contribute most directly to mutual encouragement and the upbuilding and strengthening of the Christian community.

Varieties of Gifts, but the Same Spirit

Paul begins his discussion in 1 Corinthians 12:1-3 by dealing with the criterion of possession by the Spirit. Apparently there was some unclarity on this question in Corinth. The subsequent discussion, especially in chapter 14, suggests that speaking in tongues received particular emphasis in Corinth, and it is possible that it was understood by some as the evidence that a person had been filled with the Spirit. In any case, Paul makes it clear that the particular manifestations of the Spirit are not themselves the criteria for discerning the presence of the Spirit. Analogous phenomena also occurred in other non-Christian religious communities in which they had participated (v. 2).[8] The presence and the work of the Holy Spirit is defined by the confession "Jesus is Lord," for no one can say this except by the Holy Spirit.[9] This corresponds to the general emphasis in Paul that it is the function of the Spirit to make us children of God and to drive this conviction into our hearts. Thus, when we cry "Abba! Father!" it is the Spirit himself testifying with our spirit to our sonship (cf. Rom. 8:14-17; Gal. 4:6f.). Hence the gift of the Spirit is primarily associated with faith, which the Spirit works in us, not with any of the particular manifestations of the Spirit. This corresponds to the general relationship between the use of the word *charisma* to refer to the gift of salvation itself and its use to refer to various particular gifts given to individuals or through individuals. Within the context of the confession to Jesus as Lord or to God as Father, the Spirit bestows various gifts and capacities as he wills for the good of the community. But the possession of particular gifts does not mean that one participates more fully in the Spirit, nor does a lack of these gifts mean one participates less fully in the Spirit.[10]

This is made very clear in the discussion in the remainder of the chapter (12:4-30). Verses 4-11 stress that there are varieties of gifts given by the same Spirit. Parallel expressions are "varieties of service" given by the same Lord, "varieties of working" given by the same God, and "manifestation of the Spirit." The point that Paul makes is that the Spirit gives particular gifts or manifestations to each Christian as the Spirit wills (not as we will), giving different particular gifts to different people. The purpose of all these gifts is for the common good (v. 7). They are for the sake of the entire community, not for the elevation of the person who has particular gifts. This is developed in the image of the body in vv. 12-26, which makes it clear that varieties of gifts are essential to the nature of the Christian community, and that one member ought not to yearn for the particular gifts given to another member. The gifts of the Spirit can only properly be understood when they are set within the context of the Christian community, which is one body in Christ precisely in its diversity, not in spite of it.

In understanding the relation between the gifts of the Spirit two points are emphasized in this section. The first is that the Spirit gives different gifts to various individuals as he chooses. This emphasis on the diversity of the gifts distributed to different people occurs in all of the discussions of charismatic gifts except in the letters to Timothy where it refers to the specific gift he has received (Rom. 12:6; 1 Cor. 7:7; Eph. 4:11ff.; 1 Pet. 4:10f.). The difference in the character of the lists in the different letters suggests that the kind of manifestations of the Spirit that occurred in various Christian communities also differed. This means that when 1 Corinthians 1:7 speaks of the Corinthians not lacking in any *charisma,* this is to be referred to the community, not to individuals. It must also be taken in the sense that they do not lack any *charisma* that the Spirit deems necessary for their community.

Second, the Spirit gives these gifts for the common good, i.e., for the benefit of the community as a whole, which again is an accent common to all the passages including 1 Timothy. This means not only that the differences should be recognized, but also that the gifts should be recognized as manifestations of the Spirit for the sake of the community.[11] This means that Christian love, which accepts others in their diversity and uniqueness with the differences in the manifestations of the Spirit, is the necessary horizon within which to deal adequately with the gifts of the Spirit. This is reflected by the fact that the lists of the gifts of the Spirit are closely connected with discussions of the importance of love in Romans 12:99ff.; 1 Corinthians 13; 1 Peter 4:8f. (cf. also 2 Tim. 1:6ff.). Paul apparently does not understand love as one of the *charismata* as such (cf. 1 Cor. 14:1), but as the context within which they are exercised for the benefit of the community without elevating the one or downgrading the other.

The degree to which Paul insists that the manifestations of the Spirit are for the common good and for building up the church as a whole becomes very clear in 1 Corinthians 14 where he makes a comparative evaluation of prophecy and tongues. There he sees prophecy as superior to tongues in that the former builds up, encourages, and consoles men and in this way edifies the church in contrast with tongues which edifies the individual (14:2-5). Hence, in church, rational, understandable speech is greatly preferred so that people may learn from it (vv. 19; 29-33; 39-40). This function of the gifts for the community as a whole is the reason he insists that their use be ordered in a reasonable way, which also includes ordering them in such a way that all their gifts, including tongues, are affirmed (vv. 26-33, 37-40). Thus the Corinthians, who are eager for manifestations of the

Spirit—apparently especially for the gift of tongues—must "strive to excell in building up the church" (v. 12). But in the midst of this rather critical evaluation of tongues, Paul does not negate their gift but in fact upholds its place by expressing a desire that all men speak in tongues [12] and by stressing his own exercise of the gift of tongues (vv. 5, 18). Thus, he affirms the importance of their gift as a gift of the Spirit even when he is critical of a certain kind of emphasis on it. This suggests what he said in 12:22-25 about the greater honor given to the inferior parts of the body so that there would be no discord, but the members would care for each other. Hence, he concludes the discussion by urging them to desire prophecy but not to forbid tongues (v. 39).

Paul's Experience of Spiritual Gifts

It is necessary to conclude with a brief consideration of the fundamental issue in the discussion between Paul and the Corinthians on the matter of spiritual gifts, which does not end with the writing of 1 Corinthians, but has to be taken up in new ways in 2 Corinthians 10-13.[13] The early Christian understanding that the church was a community which was caught up into the rule and glory of the resurrected and exalted Lord has already been mentioned. Ephesians 2:4-7, which may have been a part of an early baptismal liturgy, speaks of the Christian having been raised from death with Jesus and having already been enthroned with him in heavenly places (cf. 1:19-23; see also Col. 2:12-14). John 11:24-26 speaks of Jesus as the resurrection and the life, and uses the phrase "whoever lives and believes in me shall never die."

The Corinthian Christians apparently understood the Spirit as participation already in the full reality of Jesus' resurrection, so that they had already transcended life in this world with its fragmentation and brokenness. Hence, things done in this world and the powers that prevail over this world, including sin and death, no longer have any power over them. For this reason, of course, there is no future resurrection for them, since they are no longer subject to death! It is for this reason that Paul can use the fact that many of them are weak, ill, and die as evidence that they are misusing the Lord's Supper (11:27-30)—an argument that would not work unless they assumed the opposite were true if they used the sacrament properly.

In 1 Corinthians 15 the resurrection of Christ is known by both Paul and the Corinthians (vv. 3, 13f.) but what is at issue is whether they will resurrect and whether death is still a power that finally remains to be overcome (cf. esp. vv. 20-28).[14] They demonstrate their knowledge of the non-reality of idols by eating food offered to idols in the idol's temple (ch. 8, cf. v. 10), and they need to be warned against the danger of falling again under demonic powers (ch. 10). Both their sexual indulgence, of which they are proud, and their sexual abstinence (ch. 5-7) have their meaning in the conviction that they have transcended life in this world and have already entered heavenly life where there is neither marrying nor giving in marriage, but they are like the angels (e.g. Mark 12:25). Their conviction that they possess the fulfillment of all things is clear in 1 Corinthians 3:18-23; 4:6-13, where Paul sarcastically contrasts their assumed existence with his own and that of the other apostles.

After Paul wrote 1 Corinthians, the problem apparently became worse, for at least some people in Corinth seem to have then denied Paul's apostolic authority. They apparently used as evidence the fact that he did not exercise manifestations of extraordinary charismatic power among them, but that his presence and speech were weak and unimpressive (cf. 2 Cor. 10:10-12; 11:6, 7). In an extensive apology for his apostleship [15] in 2 Corinthians 10-13, he uses precisely his weakness as evidence of his apostleship. In form this is analogous to apologies in the Socratic tradition in which a person demonstrates that he is a true philosopher and not a charlatan by ironically pointing out his lack of rhetorical skill and external manifestations to commend his message. Paul appropriates this apologetic tradition to defend his apostleship and at the same time to contend that the manifestations of the Spirit do not in fact transport us beyond the fragmentedness, weakness, and brokenness of life in this world, but that the Spirit manifests the power of God precisely in the midst of this weakness (11:30; 12:9-10; 13:4, 9). Thus, Paul's experience of a miracle in his own life is one in which a healing did not occur, since God's grace was sufficient for him and God's power is made perfect in weakness (2 Cor. 12:6-10). This same emphasis on participation in the weakness of the cross as the form the power of God takes in this life in the midst of its brokenness runs throughout the Corinthian letters (cf. 1 Cor. 1:18-2:5; 4:6-13; 2 Cor. 4:7-18), and he commends this mode of existence to the Corinthians.

Power in the Midst of Weakness

Hence, the fundamental issue is whether one's understanding of Christian existence is characterized by a theology of the cross or by a theology of glory, whether God's power is experienced in this world in the midst of weakness and brokenness or in the transcendence of life in this world. Does the Spirit elevate us to some suprahuman plane of existence, or does the Spirit free us to be fully human in this world? This is really a question of the nature of the gospel itself, and whether Christian faith can be maintained only in the face of a clear recognition of the concrete realities of life in this world and of our own experience. If to be a Christian means that we must be translated beyond the weakness of life in this world, then Christianity can be maintained only in the attempt to conceal reality from ourselves, and it becomes accompanied by guilt in the face of the actuality we experience.

It is only when the Spirit frees us from our illusions about ourselves and the form of God's power in the world, that is, when he frees us to be truly human rather than freeing us from humanness, that the Spirit frees and transforms us in the midst of the reality in which we live. For Paul the Spirit does not encounter us in some transcendent realm to sustain us with his power, but he encounters and sustains us with his power in the midst of this life and its weakness and brokenness. This means that we cannot experience God's power primarily in the external circumstances of our life in a direct way, but we can experience his power only in the word of his promise which meets us in the midst of this life and upholds us and sustains us there. For he is a God who established his Lordship over us by taking into himself our weakness, our suffering, our sin, and our death in order to be with us and to give us life through his Spirit in the midst of death, righteousness in the midst of sin, and power in the midst of weakness. Within the domain of the humanness of our life in this world, all the gifts of the Spirit have their place, but they are not the transportation of men into a higher plane of existence (1 Cor. 13:8-13).

Notes

1. The longer ending in Mark (Mark 16:9-20), which is not in the oldest and best manuscripts and probably was not originally a part of the Gospel, also speaks of signs which will accompany those who believe: in Jesus' name they will cast out demons, speak in new tongues, pick up serpents, be unaffected by drinking poison, and heal the sick through laying on of hands (vv. 17f.).
2. On one level Acts 2 seems to be speaking of understandable speech in the languages of the pilgrims from various countries (v. 6). On another level, it seems to presuppose that the phenomenon was incoherent speech. The latter seems to be presupposed in the charge of drunkenness which leads into Peter's sermon, since people are not normally accused of drunkenness for understandable speech in foreign languages. This probably reflects a complex history behind the story as we now have it in Acts 2.
3. Peter's sermon in Acts 2:14ff., for example, clearly presupposes that the Spirit is poured out on all Christians in the fact that it sees the gift of the Spirit in the Christian community as the fulfillment of the prophecy in Joel 2:28ff.
4. Cf. the discussion of early Christian enthusiasm in Ernst Käsemann, *Jesus Means Freedom* (Philadelphia: Fortress Press, 1970). There are also analogous phenomena associated with possession by the Spirit in the Old Testament as well as elsewhere in the ancient Near East and the Hellenistic world. Thus, Saul was possessed by the Spirit and prophesied with the prophets (1 Sam. 10:5-13; 19:18-24). Here prophecy does not seem to have its ordinary meaning, but it apparently refers to ecstatic behavior of some sort. The work of Elijah and Elisha was associated with miraculous

power, providing a point of contact between the tradition of ecstatic prophecy and the tradition of the great Old Testament prophets. Ezekiel provides another point of contact, for in his life the Spirit also manifested itself in some rather spectacular ways. Joel 2:28-29 envisions a time at the end of history when God's Spirit would be poured out on all flesh, resulting in people prophesying, dreaming dreams, and seeing visions. Elsewhere in the Old Testament people are empowered by the Spirit for functions that are analogous to our ordinary use of the word *charisma* today, e.g. political and military leadership and the critical and supportive function of Old Testament prophecy.

5. The emphasis on the variety of gifts seems to be related to a tendency of some of the Corinthian Christians to say, "It is well for a man not to touch a woman" (7:1). They apparently have made it a principal that Christians must refrain from sexual relations, a conviction Paul rejects.
6. There are three lists in 1 Cor. 12 and a kind of list in ch. 13:

1 Cor. 12:8-10	1 Cor. 12:28	1 Cor. 12:29f.	1 Cor. 13
utterance of wisdom	apostles	apostles	tongues
utterance of knowledge	prophets	prophets	prophetic powers
faith (moves mountains?)	teachers	teachers	knowledge
gifts of healing	miracle workers	miracle workers	faith
miracle workers	gifts of healing	gifts of healing	(moves mountains)
prophecy	helpers		martyrdom
distinguishing spirits	administrators		faith
tongues	tongues	tongues	hope
interpretation (tongues)		interpretation	love

Along with the lists in Rom. and 1 Pet., we can also include the similar list in Eph. 4:11, although the gifts are not called *charismata* there:

Rom. 12:6	1 Pet. 4:10	Eph. 4:11
prophecy	speaking	apostles
service	service	prophets
teaching		evangelists
exhortation		pastors
contributing		teachers
giving aid		
doing acts of mercy		

We should also include in our field of view the fruit of the Spirit in Gal. 5:22f.: love, joy, peace, patience, kindness, goodness, faithfulness, gentleness, self-control. The general character of this list corresponds to the emphasis on love in 1 Cor. 13 as well as to the general character of the lists in Rom. 12 and 1 Pet. 4:10 and to the items included in 2 Tim. 1:6f.

7. Prophecy is not to be understood simply as analogous to preaching, although that may be a dimension of it (e.g. 1 Cor. 14:3). It also included the revelation of messages for certain people or communities, such as in Revelation or in the incident when Agabus told Paul that the Holy Spirit said he would be arrested in Jerusalem (Acts 21:11).
8. Cf. Hans Conzelmann, *Der erste Brief an die Korinther,* Kritischexegetischer Kommentar (11th ed.; Göttingen: Vandenhoeck & Ruprecht, 1969), pp. 242-244 (to ecstatic phenomena) and pp. 275-276 (for material on analogies to speaking in tongues); also F. W. Beare, "Speaking in Tongues," *Journal of Biblical Literature,* 83 (1964), 229ff.
9. There is some possibility that the phrase "Jesus be cursed!" was also used by the Corinthians in the sense of emphasizing their commitment to the exalted Lord in distinction from the human Jesus (cf. 2 Cor. 5:16), but this is not clear.
10. Where Paul does make a distinction between mature and immature Christians in 1 Cor. 3:1-4, the basis for the distinction is in their jealousy and strife and their tendency to set up factions within the Christian community.
11. It may seem difficult to understand how the gift of tongues contributes to the common good. Paul himself reflects this difficulty when he compares tongues and prophecy in 1 Cor. 14 (esp. vv. 2-5, 19, 22, 27) where he seems to regard tongues apart from the gift of interpretation as merely edifying the individual rather than the community. For that reason he restricts the use of tongues in the church. One could perhaps say that tongues does contribute to the common good in that it drives all of us to accept our unity in Christ with people who have received very different manifestations of the Spirit, thus driving us in the direction of actualizing a more diverse kind of Christian community in this and other areas as well. In any case, the person who speaks in tongues or the person who does not is not to be accepted as one with us in Christ in spite of his gift or lack of it or by suppressing the difference, but in view of the difference.
12. This is not to be taken in an absolute sense that all men really in the final analysis ought to have this gift, contradicting what he said in ch. 12 about the diversity of gifts so that not all men should speak in tongues. It rather has concessive force, and is used to affirm the importance of their gift even

while discussing it critically. If people interpret 14:5, 18 in the absolute sense that all Christians really ought to speak in tongues if they are to participate in the fullest sense in the Spirit, they would be obligated to interpret the statement in 7:7 the same way and become celibate.

13. To the situation in Corinth and Paul's relation to the community in his letters, cf. Karl Barth, *The Resurrection of the Dead,* tr. H. J. Stenning (London, 1933); R. Bultmann, "Karl Barth, *The Resurrection of the Dead,*" *Faith and Understanding,* Vol. I, tr. Louise Pettibone Smith (New York: Harper & Row, 1969), 66-94; Walter Schmithals, *Gnosticism in Corinth,* tr. John E. Steely (Nashville: Abingdon, 1971); Hans Dieter Betz, *Der Apostel Paulus und die sokratische Tradition* (Tübingen: Mohr, 1972); Hans Conzelmann, *Der erste Brief an die Korinther.* Ernst Käsemann, *Jesus Means Freedom* gives a helpful survey of the question of freedom and the manifestation of the Spirit in the early church.
14. Apparently the same problem arose in the Thessalonian church, requiring Paul to deal with the fact that Christians who have died before the return of Christ will be raised at his coming (1 Thess. 4:13ff.). 1 Tim. 2.18 criticizes people who say that the resurrection has already taken place.
15. Cf. esp. Betz, *op. cit.*

2

A Historical Perspective on Some Contemporary Religious Movements

Paul G. Sonnack
Professor of Church History
Luther Theological Seminary
St. Paul, Minnesota

Worth Study! →

2

A Historical Perspective on Some Contemporary Religious Movements

Most of those movements in the long history of the church which have tended to place primary stress on the necessity for personal religious experience or the unfettered working of the Spirit on individual persons have arisen, at least in part, in protest against formalizing and rationalizing tendencies in church and society. In the course of their own development, however, these movements have gradually adopted the same kind of formalism that they originally protested against.

The great pietistic movements of the 18th and 19th centuries, for example, emerged as reactions against orthodox formalisms. When church establishments in Great Britain, the Scandinavian countries, and on the continent of Europe tended to equate Christian life with assent to particular theological formulations or observance of particular liturgical patterns, pietists launched a vigorous and widespread protest in the interest of what they regarded as genuine Christianity. But in the process of their own development, certain patterned ways of thinking and acting manifested themselves and were accorded normative status. Hence, for example, the pietist stress on the absolute necessity for personal religious experience or the development of ethical patterns, whether legalistic or antinomian, as acceptable expressions of the ways in which the Christian life is to be ordered.

What the foregoing paragraphs are intended to suggest is that the subtle interplay of freedom and order furnishes an interpretative motif for understanding the character of some contemporary American religious movements such as revivalism, the charismatics, and the Jesus-people. All such movements seem initially to emerge out of a profound sense of dissatisfaction with contemporary demands for order, whether expressed by a highly organized technological society or by the bureaucratic structures and orthodoxies of most mainline denominations. In the name of humanity or of that which is authentically religious, they demand freedom from the confinements which order imposes. To the degree that they appeal to reservoirs of discontent with the present order of things, they generate a positive response from persons across a broad spectrum of social class, economic status, and denominational affiliation.

Hence these movements must be taken seriously. But as they flourish it becomes necessary for them to enunciate as precisely as possible the particular elements and emphases that give them their characteristic identity and then to insist on conformity to them. The revivalist commits himself to a particular technique which has far-reaching implications. The charismatic specifies the characteristics of his movement by identifying the working of the Spirit with glossolalia and the baptism of the Holy Spirit. Jesus-people require conformity to a particular interpretation of Jesus, or they insist on the necessity for a particular form of Jesus-centered piety. The point is that in the process of development new forms emerge in each of these movements, and new systems are born. The orders may be novel, but they are orders nonetheless, and conformity to them becomes requisite for membership in the group. When the quest for freedom results in the development of new systems and the demand for freedom is replaced by the demand for conformity, the movements have come full circle.

The Importance of Charles G. Finney

In a brief essay it is not possible to offer even a cursory sketch of the historical origin and development of the religious movements we have mentioned. As a concrete illustration of our theme, however, it might be both helpful and instructive to refer to a particular episode from our American religious history. Fortunately for us, the fountainhead of most contemporary movements can be located in the career of one man—Charles G. Finney. On the one hand, Finney was the progenitor and architect of modern revivalism; on the other, he gave shape, particularly in the later years of his ministry, to the perfectionist impulse that was to come to full flower in the development of the holiness movements and, in turn, the pentecostal movements which were intimately related to them. To understand Finney, then, is to gain insight into the character of most of the contemporary American religious movements with which we are here concerned.

Charles G. Finney was born in Connecticut, but he was reared in western New York State which, at that time, was frontier country—a "wilderness," as Finney himself described it. After a brief stint of teaching, he began, in 1818, to read law in a local office in Adams, New York, with the intention of becoming a lawyer. He was nearly finished with these studies when, in 1821, he was suddenly converted. This experience changed the course of his life. Abandoning a possible career as a lawyer and convinced that he had been given the mission of pulling men "out of the fire," he began immediately to preach in Adams and neighboring towns. With his commanding presence and utter sincerity, he was successful in fomenting wild revivals. As his fame spread, he was invited to one town after another in western and upper New York State, and everywhere his efforts met with great success. His own account of these early revivals in his *Memoirs* is fascinating reading.

Finney had begun his revival preaching without the benefit of formal theological training. To compensate for that lack, he soon put himself under the supervision of the presbytery in his community. The ministers who formed this august group recommended that he go to Princeton to study theology. But Finney refused to do so on the grounds that the formalisms of the theology taught at Princeton, at least as represented in the ministers he knew, were completely at variance with the understanding of the Bible he had derived from his own personal experience. Finney did consent to read theology under the tutorial supervision of the local Presbyterian minister, but that experience resulted only in controversy and had the consequence of confirming Finney in his suspicion that the structures of Presbyterian theology and church order were completely unacceptable. He chose to hew his independent way, relying primarily upon the "revelations" that had come to him from his own experience as keys which unlocked the meaning of the Bible. Eventually he incorporated his insights into his own systematic theology, a novel system which was to be widely influential in the development of American Protestantism.

More than any other single person, it was Finney who self-consciously conceived and developed revivalism as a technique, a way of doing things, of accomplishing specified ends. He was convinced that if only the right means were employed, the desired results would be achieved. In systematic fashion, for he always retained the lawyer's penchant for order, he developed what came to be known as the "new measures." These new measures were simply the means employed by the revivalist, the use of a repertoire of devices like the protracted meeting and the "anxious bench," in order to elicit a decision. Finney did not invent these measures, but since he had an almost inordinate confidence in their effectiveness he adopted them and perfected their use. It was because he championed the use of these measures that Finney was opposed so vehemently by the more conservative Congregational and Presbyterian ministers. They regarded the use of these measures as an odious and tasteless reversion to barbarism. In response to their criticism, Finney simply asserted that "they worked." They achieved results. And that is an argument which pragmatic Americans have always found difficult to resist.

In 1834, after almost ten years as an itinerant revivalist,

Finney accepted the invitation to become the pastor of the Broadway Tabernacle in New York City. In 1835, he also accepted the responsibility of serving as Professor of Theology at Oberlin College for a part of each year. For several years thereafter he divided his time between his work as pastor in the tabernacle and as professor in the college. Eventually he was to become president of Oberlin. His decision to accept these positions after the busy years of itinerant revivalism marked an important turning-point in his career. He had expended all of his considerable powers for ten years in the effort to win converts, but he had manifested virtually no concern for what happened to them once the revival had ended. He had concentrated so exclusively on the use of those measures that would produce results that he had given no thought to living the Christian life which should follow conversion. As the pastor of a congregation he could no longer avoid this question, and there is some evidence that he soon became more than a little skeptical about the lasting effects of his efforts as a revivalist.

He began now to give serious consideration to the nature of the Christian life, and he came to the conclusion that there were two possibilities. On the one hand, the convert could press on to what Finney called "entire sanctification." He could, that is to say, achieve holiness by living in perfect obedience to the law of God. On the other hand, and more importantly, the convert could, as Finney put it, "aim at being useful in the highest degree possible." That is to say, he could involve himself with his whole strength and devotion in those activities that would be of some benefit to his fellow man. Out of the former possibility was generated the impulse which gave birth to a plethora of perfectionist sects and eventually came to full bloom in the development of the holiness-pentecostal movements.

Out of the counsel of benevolent activity as the fruit of conversion was generated the participation of his converts in the reform movements of the time, particularly the temperance and anti-slavery movements. In an important study, entitled *The Antislavery Impulse,* Gilbert Barnes has maintained that the leadership of the anti-slavery movement in the United States was provided by men like Theodore Dwight Weld and others who had been converted in Finney's revivals.

Finney's lifetime spanned the first half of the 19th century, one of the most creative epochs in American history. He stood astride the period as "the representative" of American revivalism. More than that, he exemplified in his ministry precisely those elements that have come to characterize those religious movements we are trying to understand. It would be an over-simplification, of course, to maintain that these contemporary movements stand in direct historical continuity with Finney. Historical development is more complex than that. To a striking degree, nonetheless, Finney did articulate a stance and a style that is repeated in many contemporary religious movements in America. An understanding of Finney, therefore, is significant in the shaping of our perspective on the present situation. A number of indications can be specified

The Problem of Structure

For one thing, the initial shape of Finney's ministry was engendered in protest against the established structures of a church system he found to be unacceptable. Since the theological propositions enunciated by the ministers he knew did not jibe with the understanding of the Bible he derived from his own experience, he refused to be cast into the Princeton mold. In his early preaching, as is indicated in his *Memoirs,* he went to considerable lengths to specify precisely those doctrines he regarded as unpalatable. He rejected, for example, the Calvinist insistence on the sovereignty of God in favor of the absolute necessity of man's decision in the process of his redemption from sin. Throughout a long and exceedingly fruitful ministry, Finney maintained a stance of protest against a benighted church system, and he claimed the freedom to do so out of a deep concern for what he regarded as genuinely religious.

Such protests usually possess a claim to legitimacy. Order and system are necessary in church and society insofar as they contribute to human ends. We would not be able to live together without them. But they can become demonic when they are transposed into goals which demand human subservience. That is why protests against them in the name of human freedom should be seriously examined. Most of the contemporary religious movements in the United States have arisen in protest against the lethargy and indifference that characterize the religious involvement in the mainline denominations. It may be that these protests also emerge as an indictment against the blandness and mechanization of life in a highly organized and rigid technological society. Whatever their source, the movements should be taken seriously insofar as they are significant attempts to reclaim for human life the elements of freedom and spontaneity.

But protests against systems of order are never launched in a vacuum. Whether he wants to or not, the critic expresses his own point of view, and he does so precisely in his critique of other points of view. Protests against particular manifestations of order usually enunciate a preference for some other form of order. Thus while critiques and protests must be taken seriously, they must also themselves he subjected to serious critical scrutiny. Finney's critique of Presbyterian doctrine, for example, was significant and proved to be vastly influential in the development of American Protestant theology. But it did not emerge from a standpoint of neutrality. It was developed out of Finney's preference for a particular version of the doctrine of the freedom of man's will in relation to the sovereignty of God. As such, it may have been an important attempt to reclaim for Christian theology a significant emphasis that had been virtually lost in the structures of the New England theology which Finney knew, but it was itself a partial view which could not claim exemption from critical assessment.

The same point can be made with respect to the varieties of protest articulated by current religious movements. As protests against particular structures, they express a preference for different sets of order. It is one thing, for example, to sense the release engendered by the ecstatic experience; it is quite another to insist that the ecstatic experience is the essence of religion. It is one thing to experience healing; it is quite another to make healing a normative criterion for all true religion. To substitute one structure for another may be helpful, at times even essential; but it ought never to suggest that the new form should be exempted from the rigorous evaluation which has been applied to the old. We seem somehow to be trapped in a dilemma from which there is no escape. We seek freedom from the dominance of order only to discover that the new forms we have accepted are as confining and restricting as the old forms we have discarded. Like the man in Jesus' story, we may even discover that the unclean spirit which is driven out to wander in the desert may return with seven other spirits more wicked than himself and that "the last state of that man becomes worse than the first."

The Individual and the Community

There was another element in Finney's purview which seems to recur in some contemporary religious movements, and that was the importance he attached to individual decision and action. The consequence was a radical individualizing of religious experience, so radical, that the reality of the corporate or the community was virtually ignored. This preoccupation was reflected in Finney's view of the church. He regarded the church simply as a voluntary organization made up of those who by their own individual decisions agree to form a congregation. The implication was that by their individual choices men create the church; the church does not exist prior to such individual decisions. To put the point succinctly: Finney's doctrine of the church was based on the presumption that the individual is prior to the community; hence he was unable to see that the community might be prior to the individual.

The same individualistic bias was also reflected in Finney's counsel of benevolent activity as the fruit of conversion. As he understood it, benevolence was a concrete expression of the concern one individual might have for another, or that a group of individuals might manifest towards other individuals. By no stretch of the imagination was the counsel of benevolence to be extended to the community itself. To be sure, some of Finney's converts did so extend the notion, particularly by their involvement in the anti-slavery movement, but Finney did not approve. Rather he expressed the suspicion that such involvements were dangerous innovations insofar as they moved away from the individualistic basis of benevolence.

The tendency towards individualism is also present in some of the current American religious movements. It can be detected in the cults of healing. In their view, it is the individual who receives healing. They would regard as preposterous any suggestion that religion might have something to do with the healing of the many sicknesses endemic to the life of communities. The individualistic bias is also clearly expressed in the activities of the current revivalists. Now as in the days of Finney, the revivalist's appeal is the call for individual decision. All the paraphernalia in the technical arsenal of the revivalist is employed in the attempt to produce that end. And once it is achieved the work of revivalist is ended. To be sure, he may encourage his converts to affiliate with some religious community and may even develop some devices by which to facilitate it. But insofar as he is not himself responsible to any religious community he recognizes no obligation to concern himself with the essential corporate dimensions of the religious life.

When the revivalist articulates his understanding of the religious life, he usually reveals his individualistic preoccupation. When he counsels charity to the neighbor as a fruit of conversion he means that the individual should do what he can to ameliorate his distress. It would not occur to him that faith might find legitimate expression by the Christian's involvement in the problems of the social order.

The Nature of Ministry

A third point of emphasis where the relationship between Finney and some contemporary religious movements seems clear has to do with what may be called the technologizing of ministry. As we have noted previously, Finney adopted and perfected the use of the "new-measures," so-called, because he was convinced that the "right use" of means would inevitably produce the desired results. It is noteworthy that the conservative ministers who opposed Finney were moved to do so not because they lacked confidence in the effectiveness of means but rather because they resented the frontier crudeness of the measures Finney employed. The presumption that ministry *is* essentially a technical enterprise has found wide acceptance in American Protestantism, so much so that as a form of ministry (an "order," if you please) it has tended to replace the classical form of ministry as an office of gospel proclamation. In the view of many Protestants, the pastor has become a technician.

It is ironic that those contemporary religious movements which protest against rationalizing and technologizing tendencies in church and society should themselves unwittingly adopt the view that ministry is technique. That they have done so is virtually beyond dispute. The presumption that ministry is to be equated with the deployment of technique has been accepted by almost all revivalists. In his *Lectures on Revivals of Religion,* first published in 1835, Finney produced the handbook on the technique of revivalism which ever since has been regarded as authoritative by a succession of great American revivalists—Dwight L. Moody, Billy Sunday, and Billy Graham. Whatever else it may be, revivalism is essentially a technique. The semi-documentary film, *Marjoe,* is a persuasive statement of the point. Whatever one may make of Marjoe's confession of insincerity and lack of integrity, he is crystal clear in his understanding of ministry: ministry is technique and nothing but technique! And he knows that his sincerity or lack thereof has nothing whatsoever to do with the smoothness and effectiveness of his technical virtuosity as a revivalist.

Contemporary cults of healing and also the charismatic movement have tended to equate ministry with technique. This allegation will be vigorously disputed by practitioners, of course, but some not entirely impartial observation of the phenomena gives credence to it. Those who practice what is called "divine healing" insist that they are but passive instruments in the hands of God. But they have adopted a variety of techniques which are designed to produce the desired results. The charismatics, too, seem to have learned their lessons from the revivalists. Their presumption seems to be that the work of the Holy Spirit, as manifested in glossolalia and the baptism of the Spirit, is somehow dependent on a context of expectancy which has been built up by the skillful employment of a variety of techniques.

The question of the relation of technique to ministry

is, of course, a very subtle one. It is one thing, however, to insist that technique is inevitably involved in the doing of ministry; it is quite another to equate ministry with the deployment of technique. Preoccupation with the latter flirts with danger, if not with disaster, at two points. First of all, as Finney himself came to realize when he accepted the responsibilities of a settled pastor, primary concentration on means tends to blunt careful consideration of ends. It is never sufficient to be able simply to do something or to make things work. One must always inquire about the adequacy and appropriateness of the purpose for which a thing is done. The question of purpose leads inevitably to a serious and critical consideration of beginnings and ends, about the context in which something is done as well as the end for which something is done. There is little indication that the technician pays sufficient attention to such a question. A second point, related to the first, is that the technician is always manipulative in his relation to his subjects. Such an operation may be relatively harmless when it is applied to inert materials like steel and wood, but when it is applied to human persons it verges on obscenity.

The Status of Theological Systems

A fourth and final point of comparison can be made. It has to do with the enunciation and maintenance of theological perspective. Finney was unique among American revivalists insofar as he did take the trouble, once he ceased his itinerancy, to explicate his own theological point of view (Cf., his *Lectures on Systematic Theology,* first published in 1846). In this work he was primarily concerned to explain and justify his views on the doctrine of entire sanctification as the natural result of his activities as a revivalist. There are indications that his work was influential in the movement of American theology from New England Calvinism to the Liberalism which flourished in the 19th century.

Most contemporary religious movements, by contrast, seem to regard the theological enterprise either with indifference or suspicion. It is relatively easy to understand why this is the case with the revivalist. In his appeal for decisions it is necessary for him to reduce all ambiguities to two simple alternatives. Hence he always tends to oversimplify complex issues and problems. Moreover, in his eagerness to "get results" the revivalist usually manifests a crusty impatience with theological questions. He tends instead to sanction the pragmatic axiom: "that is true which gets results." In terms of this test he justifies the means he employs. And the pragmatic axiom tends also to become the criterion by which he judges doctrinal affirmations. The consequence is not only that he usually accepts any idea that can pass the pragmatic test but also that he is deprived thereby of the possibility of developing a clearly articulated perspective for making theological and moral judgments on the ideologies and practices of his society. This fact helps us to understand why the revivalist is usually inclined to accept in uncritical fashion the ideas and customs that prevail in the popular culture. He does not take the initiative in trying to give shape to the culture; rather he reflects what the popular culture seems to dictate. While the revivalist manifests a remarkable adaptability in relation to technological advances, he generally exhibits neither the desire nor an aptitude for fundamental theological questions. Where he does not ignore such questions, or shy away from them, he tends to regard them as a positive threat to Christian faith and life and defends himself against them by hiding behind bastions of obscurantism.

It is less easy to understand why the charismatic movement seems also to manifest a similar impatience with theology. Since it does center in an intense preoccupation with the work of the Holy Spirit, one might have expected it to develop a powerful theological perspective around this central theme. Such a contribution could be of immense significance to the church. Perhaps such a perspective will be produced in the foreseeable future. It has not yet appeared. That is the case presumably because the charismatic movement in its present manifestations seems to be more concerned with the immediacy of experience than it does with theological reflection on that experience. This fact may also account for the reductionist tendencies and defensive tone of the theological statements which charismatics have thus far produced.

Summary

My purpose has been to develop a historical perspective on some contemporary religious movements in the United States. It has been suggested, on the one hand, that these movements have emerged initially as protests against the orders that prevail in church and society, particularly as they are expressed in such questions as the relation of individual to community, the nature of ministry, and the status of theological systems. Insofar as religious communities tend to bind religious life and expression to inherited modes, they inhibit the freedom which faith engenders. Protests against such tendencies are necessary and must be taken with utmost seriousness. It has also been suggested, however, that in the interest of providing continuity for their own predilections, movements of protest move quickly and decisively to the development of constitutive patterns. Consideration of such structures makes it clear that they run the danger of foreshortening classical Christian witness.

It is not possible to predict the future. It is to be hoped, however, that it will be possible to avoid unhealthy conflict between different types of order. But that will be possible only to the degree that an atmosphere of mutual openness and respect can be made to prevail.

3

The Sociology of Charismatic Movements

Johannes A. Schiller
Professor of Sociology
Pacific Lutheran University
Tacoma, Washington

3

The Sociology of Charismatic Movements

Sociology has its own conceptual and methodological approach to religious behavior and religious systems. The apostle Paul said, "We have this treasure in earthen vessels." It is the behavior and organization of "earthen vessels" that sociology attempts to describe and understand. Religious systems have many of the same characteristics and features as other social systems. Therefore, sociology examines the culture, society groups, and interaction systems and processes within which religious systems function, as well as the characteristics of religious systems and their interaction with groups, systems, society and culture.

Examining charismatic movements through the eyes of sociology should provide insight into their development, structure, and functions. However, it does not make it possible for us to say why a person chooses to join charismatic movements. Many forces influence the person to associate with a particular charismatic experience as a way to satisfy his personal needs. Culture and/or subcultures, institutional relationships, group interaction patterns, and personality processes need to be examined if a more complete explanation is to be had. This chain of relationships could be illustrated in the following model; culture↔subculture↔group interaction↔psychological needs ↔group interaction↔subculture↔charismatic affiliation, to trace the process of dissaffiliation from traditional human systems to affiliation with the charismatic movement. Flacks, (1971) demonstrated how this works in the development of the youth counter culture and we find it useful for understanding the development of charismatic movements.

Our presentation will concentrate primarily on the way in which culture and social systems influence the development and nature of charismatic movements. For it is the case that certain social environments are more conducive to charismatic movements.

Sociological studies show that sectarianism, as a nontraditional religious response, develops when certain segments of society are not integrated into society or when society is in a state of confusion. For example, when groups of people are prevented from achieving the goals established by society, they become alienated. One way to respond to such a situation is to withdraw into some group activity that separates people from the mainstream of society. It provides an opportunity to belong to a significant group and to find personal satisfaction in the group's experience. Sectarian religious experiences and groups provide such a withdrawal (Yinger, 1970). "The last root of all sectarianism lies in the alienation of some group from the inclusive society within which it has to carry on its life" (Stark, 1967, Vol. 2, p. 5).

Present American culture provides opportunities for the development of charismatic behavior systems and provides individuals with social experiences and group identifications that make participation in charismatic experiences a viable alternative.

The Social Environment

American society has been described in various ways. It has been described as 1) normless, 2) massive, 3) pluralistic, and 4) bureaucratic and technological. Each of these conceptualizations helps us to understand a set of specific facets of contemporary American society and culture.

1. The anomie theory suggests the use of the idea of normlessness. Society is in an anomic state when there is a) excessive competition or conflict between groups, values, beliefs, and wills; b) ineffective, corrupt government with unscrupulous, self-interested leadership; c) an absence of common values; d) a breakdown of social control; and e) an excessive tolerance of deviancy (Winslow, 1970).

Persons and groups living in such a culture often respond with feelings of powerlessness, meaninglessness, distrust, cynicism, futility, depression, diffuse hostility, and hopelessness (Merton, 1957). Some call this alienation. Anomic conditions foster responses of aggressive retaliation, withdrawal, and resignation.

2. American society is moving from a mass society to a pluralistic society. Charismatic behavior is fostered by conditions existing in both kinds of society. Mass society is described by Daniel Bell as one in which there is

greater independence among people, estrangement of people from one another, and broken family and community ties. Ancient parochial faiths are questioned; few underlying values exist, mores and morals are in flux; and relations between individuals are tangential or compartmentalized. Each person is faced with a multiplicity of roles requiring successful performance. He argues that persons experience anxiety, a loss of self-awareness, and security. As he puts it, "there ensues a search for new faiths. The stage is set for the charismatic leader, the secular messiah, who by bestowing upon each person the semblance of necessary grace, and of fullness of personality, supplies a substitute for the older unifying belief that the mass society has destroyed" (Bell, 1961, pp. 21-22).

3. A pluralistic society creates independent groups of people through which individuals find meaningful experience, belongingness, support to legitimize their values and norms of behavior, and avenues through which to achieve their goals. Belonging to and participating in the larger society are no longer essential as the primary source of identification. People have many commitments to diverse and autonomous groups (Kornhauser, 1959). The stage has been set to legitimize diverse subcultures and to provide the means and the opportunity, through mass media and mobility, for persons with similar needs and feelings to interact and form groups that diverge from traditional value systems and life styles.

4. A technocratic society is one in which organizational integration has reached its peak. Everything aspires to become purely technical and the prime goal is scientific efficiency. Cartesian logic dominates thought and bureau-

cratic structures provide the setting for relationships (Roszak, 1968). Technocratic society, if it is to succeed, requires new values, new motivational patterns, new rights, new institutions, and new social roles. Conflict develops with the existing culture and institutions precipitating a cultural crisis. People, especially youth, regard this culture as confusing and undesirable. It becomes difficult to find meaning in life or to accept the answers given by existing institutions (Flack, 1971). Alienation from all that society and culture represent and mean develops an alienation that "deadens man's sensitivity to man" (Roszak, 1969, p. 58). So man seeks new associations that provide emotional, non-Cartesian, and communal relationships reflecting new values and norms of behavior.

Accompanying a rapidly changing culture is intergenerational discontinuity. In our technocratic society which values education, adolescence has been elongated from 3 years to 15 years. Young people are defined socially as non-adults much longer than physical or mental growth requires and are refused functional or structural identity with adult roles and institutions. This also contributes to alienation from the larger adult society and drives the young person out of his parent's world. He thus seeks identity and meaning among his peers (Eisenstadt, 1960).

In a bureaucratic society such as this people feel anomia. They feel that community leaders are detached from or indifferent to their needs, that the social order is fickle and unpredictable, that the country's moral fiber is flabby, and that immediate personal relations are no longer predictable or supportive (Srole, 1956).

The Religious Situation

Sociologists like Weber, Becker, Yinger, and Berger have shown that religious denominations reflect the same characteristics found in other social institutions. This means, for our culture, that religious denominations reflect and support the secularization of the last 200 years. They are rationalistic in their thought modes, bureaucratic in their organization, and technocratic in their efficiency. Since we have no state religion, religious diversity exists. It has been demonstrated that this diversity is as prevalent within a specific denomination as across denominations (Glock and Stark, 1966). Therefore contemporary religion betrays the anomic, massive, pluralistic, technocratic characteristics permeating the larger society.

The conditions in American society described above provide fertile ground for non-traditional forms of religious expression. "Cults and sects like other new religious movements are most likely to arise out of rapid social change, the disturbance of value systems, and conditions of religious liberty produced by religious heterogeneity" (Williams, 1970, pp. 377-378).

Looking at the functions that religion provides gives us further insight into man's search for some religious meaning in life. Sociologists state that religion provides or satisfies the following needs of people: 1) uncertainty or contingency in important events; 2) ultimate powerlessness in terms of man's environment; 3) scarcity leading to frustration and deprivation; 4) importance and difficulty of social integration; 5) security and a firm sense of identity; and 6) a way of facing the potential problems of frustration, evil, and meaning in life. If then religious experience fails to perform these functions it is no surprise that non-traditional religious experiences and organizations are created. For such persons and groups charismatic experiences provide an avenue for achieving meaning in life, for developing personal identity, and for creating interpersonal support and security.

Charismatic Movements

Sectarian movements in the past have grown out of a repudiation of the existing religious institutions. But the degree of repudiation differed for the various social classes in America. Among the lower classes, economic hardships and social injustices bred feelings of alienation toward social institutions, including the church. In contrast, the middle classes repudiated existing religious systems because of "feelings of inadequacy, confusion of standards in a highly mobile world, guilt and physical pain" (Yinger, 1970, p. 272).

Today charismatic expressions are occurring within existing religious denominations and in newly developing sectarian groups or communities. Given the paucity of extensive research, one can only attempt educated calculations on the basis of a few studies about the generating forces operating in each of the two areas.

It seems that for some middle class members of traditional denominations having feelings of inadequacy, being confused by the changing values and norms of the sacred and secular world, being dissatisfied in their work roles, and being distressed about discrepancies between the expectations and achievements of life's goals there exists a need for some kind of extra-ordinary security and assurance not presently perceived by them in existing religious institutions. Speaking in tongues, for example, provides an alternative for identity, meaning, and security for them. Ralph Lane's (1972) examination of the Charismatic Renewal Movement, a part of the Catholic Pentecostal Movement, validates this kind of postulation.

A number of young people and younger adults have joined charismatic groups. Religious communes, the Children of God, the Jesus People, and the Jesus Freaks are the more publicized charismatic groups. Phil Tracy, Robert L. Adams and Robert J. Fox, and John P. Leary have studied some of these groups. Adams and Fox (1972) report that participants are middle class teenagers and young adults. The young adults have opted out of the drug culture. Leadership in the movement is anti-establishment, rejecting the theological positions and social stance of the major Protestant denominations. Persons have joined to find peer group approval and to resolve an identity crisis. Life in the Jesus movement is ruled by the Bible and the possession of the Holy Spirit. The movement manifests spiritual sensateness, simplistic morality, anti-intellectualism, authoritarianism, withdrawal from the world, a cure-all for everything, and a very personal experience.

Leary maintains that young people who are involved in what he calls "creative disaffiliation" are prompted by a deep religious hunger. In their search they are yearning for some great transcendent experience growing out of a passion "against sameness, the uneventful, reiterative clog of time, stupid duration, and a passion for something so big and so fine that it can't be uttered" (Leary, 1972, p. 288). It is interesting that Leary as well as Adams and

Fox find relationships between the "drug trip" and the "Jesus trip."

Cultic forms of religious expression have a mystical dimension. Through them participants are replacing a fragmented secularized set of human institutional and societal relationships with a sacralized wholistic social and religious experience and personal identity. The whole of life is permeated with sacredness. Bloy (1969) reports that Karl Garrison's study of student activists shows that when secular values become dominant in a given culture, a quest for the sacred often becomes manifest in its youth. And Bloy (1969, pp. 656-657) says that "the youth of the counter culture having broken with the individualistic, rationalistic, skeptical tradition of the last 300 years in favor of a communal, personalist, 'committed' life style, now instinctively search for sacral foundations to sustain and celebrate their new identity. This quest for the sacred in an old amalgam of eastern and western terms is in itself another sign of how deeply alienated from the immediate cultural tradition the counter culture actually is."

Since basic institutions of society reflect society's anomic state, institutions like religion and the family lose some of their authority and primary group functions. Charismatic groups provide authority in religion and surrogate primary relationships in place of the family.

Roszak (1968, p. 439) comments that "what began with Zen has now rapidly, perhaps too rapidly proliferated into a phantasmagoria of exotic religiosity." Many of the cultic groups are heterogeneous yet develop a communal solidarity. They isolate themselves from outside social relationships, their own group becoming a total way of life. Cultic groups have very implicit rules and live under a charismatic leadership. The group is motivated and held together through affective relationships that provide personal psychic dividends (Pfautz, 1955).

Adams and Fox (1972) as a result of their research expressed concern and criticism about cultic groups. They claim that these movements are becoming victims of reactionary right-wing politics. They are a "cop-out" from the real world of social change and from societal problems. They deny the "psycho-socio-sexual" complexity of human nature. Their other-worldliness causes them to repudiate the world. There is a wide gap between the beliefs and ideas of the leaders and their followers.

Conclusions

We have observed that the primary factors of economic hardship and deprivation experienced by the lower classes in earlier American society are no longer adequate to describe the cultural conditions related to the development of charismatic movements. Though the lower classes are still attracted to charismatic groups, today middle class teenagers, young adults, and older people are also attracted to these forms of religious expression.

Contemporary American culture is in an anomic state, has mass society characteristics, is moving toward a pluralistic society, and is being directed by a secularized technocratic values system. Traditional religious systems and organizations reflect many of the same characteristics.

Under such conditions some people are unable to tolerate the accompanying loneliness, and the meaninglessness and uncertainty in the midst of changing and contradictory values systems. Alienation toward society has grown because of a widening gap between expectations and achievements. Self-alienation has developed as a result of fragmentation of human experience and frustration in interpersonal relationships. Young people have felt all of these conflicts and contradictions but are having the additional experience of living in an elongated, confusing no man's land between childhood and adulthood which has led them to seek a complete overthrow of established values, norms, and institutions.

They are seeking a wholeness of existence that gives affective security, personhood and community—a sacralization of all of life and the total person. Charismatic experiences and movements are one avenue of seeking such meaning and belonging. Persons having related needs and seeking similar solutions engage in a collective enterprise and produce charismatically filled experiences, relationships, and structures—the charismatic movement.

BIBLIOGRAPHY

Adams, Robert J., and Robert J. Fox. "Mainlining Jesus: The New Trip." *Society,* (February 1972), 50-56.

Barber, Bernard, "Acculturation and Messianic Movements." *American Sociological Review,* 6 (October 1941), 663-669.

Bell, Daniel. *The End of Ideology.* New York: The Free Press, 1961.

Bloy, Myron B., Jr. "Alienated Youth, the Counter Culture and the Chaplain," in *The Religious Situation,* Donald R. Cutler, ed. Boston: Beacon Press, 1969.

Durkheim, Emile. *The Elementary Forms of the Religious Life.* Trans. by Joseph W. Swain. New York: The Free Press, 1947.

Eisenstadt, S. N. *From Generation to Generation: Age Groups and Social Structure.* Glencoe: The Free Press, 1960.

Festinger, Leon and Riecken, Henry. *When Prophecy Fails.* Minneapolis: University of Minnesota Press, 1956.

Flacks, Richard. *Youth and Social Change.* Chicago: Markham Publishing Company, 1971.

Glock, Charles and Rodney Stark. *Christian Beliefs and Anti-Semitism.* New York: Harper and Row, 1966.

———. *Religion and Society in Tension.* Chicago: Rand McNally & Company, 1965.

Johnson, Benton. "Do Holiness Sects Socialize in Dominant Values?" *Social Forces,* 39 (May 1961), 309-316.

———. "On Church and Sect." *American Sociological Review,* 28 (August 1963), 539-549.

———. "Ascetic Protestantism and Political Preference." Public Opinion Quarterly, 26 (Spring 1962), 35-46.

Kornhauser, William. *The Politics of Mass Society.* New York: The Free Press, 1959.

Lane, Ralph, Jr. "A Catholic Pentecostal Prayer Meeting: An Ethnography of Control Mechanisms." Paper presented at the Annual Meeting of the Pacific Sociological Association, Portland, Oregon, April 15, 1972.

Leary, John P., S. J. "The Revolution in Religion: A Religious Breakthrough," in *Values in Conflict: A Text Reader in Social Problems.* Victor B. Ficker and James M. Rigterink. Lexington, Massachusetts: D. C. Heath and Company, 1972.

Lenski, Gerhard. *The Religious Factor: A Sociological Study of Religion's Impact on Politics, Economics, and Family Life.* Garden City, N.Y.: Doubleday & Company, Inc., 1961.

Merton, Robert K. *Social Theory and Social Structure,* rev. and enlarged ed. London: Collier-Macmillan Ltd., 1957.

Nettler, Gwinn. "Antisocial Sentiment and Criminality." *American Sociological Review,* 24 (April 1959), 202-208.

Pfautz, Harold W. "The Sociology of Secularization: Religious Groups." *American Journal of Sociology,* 61 (September 1955), 121-128.

Pope, Liston. *Millhands and Preachers.* New Haven, Conn.: Yale University Press, 1942.

Tracy, Phil. "The Jesus Freaks." *Commonweal,* (October 30, 1970), 122-125.

Roszak, Theodore. "Politics of the Nervous System." *The Nation* (April 1, 1968), 439-443.

———. "Youth and the Great Refusal." *The Nation,* (March 25, 1968), 400-407.

———. *The Making of a Counter Culture.* Garden City, N.Y.: Anchor Books, Doubleday and Company, Inc., 1969.

Seeman, Melvin. "The Logic and Limits of Mass Society Theory," unpublished paper delivered at the University of California at Los Angeles, 1963.

———. "On the Meaning of Alienation." *American Sociological Review,* 24 (December 1959), 783-791.

Srole, Leo. "Social Integration and Certain Corollaries, an Exploratory Study." *American Sociological Review,* 21 (December 1956), 709-716.

Stark, Werner. *The Sociology of Religion: A Study of Christendom,* Vol. 2. New York: Fordham University Press, 1967.

Weber, Max. *The Protestant Ethic and the Spirit of Capitalism.* Trans. by Talcott Parsons. London: George Allen and Unwin, Ltd., 1930.

Williams, Robin. *American Society: A Sociological Interpretation,* Third Edition. New York: Alfred A. Knopf, 1970.

Winslow, Robert W. *Society in Transition: A Social Approach to Deviancy.* New York: The Free Press, 1970.

Yinger, J. Milton. *Religion in the Struggle for Power: A Study in the Sociology of Religion.* Durham, N.C.: Duke University Press, 1946.

———. "Religion and Society: Problems of Integration and Pluralism Among the Privileged," in Knudton, Richard D., *The Sociology of Religion: An Anthology.* New York: Appleton-Century-Crofts, 1967.

———. *The Scientific Study of Religion.* New York: The Macmillan Company, 1970.

Seefp

4

Six Behavioral Observations about Speaking in Tongues

John P. Kildahl
Consulting Psychologist
New York, N.Y.

4

Six Behavioral Observations about Speaking in Tongues

An LSD user once told me that if I hadn't tried it, I couldn't knock it. Nothing could compare with the unfathomable beauty of a leaf rustling in the wind when on an LSD trip, he said. And the true, inner nature of a Beethoven symphony could only be grasped completely when using LSD. And again my friend reminded me, "If you haven't experienced it, you can't knock it."

This leads me to *several observations* about speaking in tongues:

Observation One: Subjective experience alone cannot determine the value of a thing. I largely discount the glowing accounts of subjective feelings as determining anything about the spiritual validity of glossolalia. Positive subjective feelings can be produced in an infinite number of ways, and the subjective experience cannot alone determine the value of any phenomenon.

Observation Two: There are five steps in the process of inducing someone to speak in tongues. These five steps closely parallel the essential steps for religious healing to take place. (See Jerome D. Frank, *Persuasion and Healing.*) From a psychological point of view, the first step seems to involve some kind of magnetic relationship between the leader and the one who is about to attempt to speak in tongues. Second, the initiate generally has a sense of personal distress—usually involving a profound life crisis. Third, the initiate has been taught a rationale for understanding what tongue-speaking is. Fourth, the presence of a supporting group of fellow believers enhances the possibility of eventually speaking in tongues. Fifth, somewhere in the process there is an intense emotional atmosphere. In a few paragraphs, let us explore further these five steps.

There are exceptions to every rule, of course, but these five conditions seem clearly evident in the testimonies of hundreds of tongue speakers. See, for example, John Sherrill's account of his own initial tongue-speaking experience in his book, *They Speak with Other Tongues.* A core aspect in a trusting dependency on a leader. This is a complex issue, that receives a more complete description in my book, *The Psychology of Speaking in Tongues.* An interesting converse to this rule is illustrated by the case of a minister who was actually in the middle of preaching a sermon against tongue-speaking when he suddenly broke out into speaking in tongues himself. Actually, a belligerent skeptic may be quite susceptible to the experience—which is an example of the psychological mechanism called reaction formation. In Shakespeare's words "Methinks he protesteth too much" may well indicate an underlying desire to conform.

The pre-tongue-speaking crises I have observed often involve a fundamental shaking of one's personal and professional identity, with a loss of meaning and purpose for one's existence. The onset of glossolalia then becomes a focus for one's life, with a sense of dependence on that experience, almost as a reason for one's being. Psychologically, it appears at times that glossolalia serves as the central confirming experience of one's existence.

The comradeship of the group provides warm acceptance as well as a rationale that the strange sounds of tongue-speaking are not babble, but a special gift. Some groups and leaders are naturally more effective than others in providing the heightened emotional atmosphere which is effective in inducing the first tongue-speaking experience. These activities often generate intense emotional feeling, sometimes even to the point of great fatigue or exhaustion. The advent of tongue-speaking is then all the more euphoric. It is my observation that when one first begins to speak in tongues when alone, these five conditions have been present in the days or weeks preceding the initial experience.

Observation Three: The feelings of well-being which accompany tongue-speaking are caused by the belief that this is an act of God's intervention in one's speech, and not by the act of the tongue-speaking itself. The actual verbalizing is a neutral experience; it is one's belief that this is a gift of God which brings an experience of euphoria. Additionally, one is helped to feel good about the experience as one is taught by others that this is indeed the very evidence of God's Spirit at work in oneself. Whenever there appeared to be a tongue-speaker who became alienated from his leader or his group, the experience of glossolalia no longer seemed to be particularly meaningful to him.

Four other occasions of glossolalia type speech should be noted.

1. There are numerous former members of the pentecostal movement who retain the ability to speak in tongues, even though they have no belief that their speech is a gift of God. Speaking in this way no longer makes them feel good as it once did when they were believing members of a pentecostal group.

2. Glossolalia is a common practice for Hindus.

3. A linguist has reported that he has been able to teach a classroom of students to speak in tongues—without reference to any religious beliefs about it.

4. An actress once explained to me that verbal expression without using a known language was an important part of the training in her acting classes. She proceeded to speak a "language" for me which sounded exactly like glossolalia. She spoke somewhat different "languages" when she was asked to express joy, or warmth, or intensity, or sadness.

To repeat, it is not the speech itself, but rather the belief about what the speech is, that makes glossolalists feel good.

Observation Four: Having observed this experience in many contexts, my conviction is that speaking in tongues should be evaluated by a community criterion: does it edify the community of believers, the church? A religious experience should measure itself by its fruits, and not simply by how it makes one feel.

The positive fruits which I have often observed among glossolalists include a greater intensity of Christian faith, a greater sense of personal power, more boldness in interpersonal relations, and increased effectiveness in being a productive person. However nebulous it may be to measure, it appears that most glossolalists evidence a greater love for mankind than before their tongues experience.

Among the negative fruits of the tongue-speaking experience that I have observed, the following should be mentioned: a somewhat mechanistic dependency on a leader; a divisive influence in many congregations; some rather histrionic displays of emotion and behavior; a subtle arrogance that one is specially singled out by God, with a tacit implication that one is somewhat beyond criticism from those who have not had the same experience; and, in my opinion, a tendency toward a simplistic theology and a literalistic view of Scripture.

Observation Five: In regard to the interpretation of tongues it should be noted that there is no recorded instance of a person speaking a foreign language which he or she has not learned through normal channels. Playing the same section of recorded tongue-speaking to two or more different interpreters of tongues reveals that no two interpreters arrive at the same interpretation. One interpreter might say that the speaker is praising God for the blessings of good health, and another interpreter might say that the speaker is praying for an answer about which of two job offers he should accept.

Observation Six: The fact that most tongue-speakers were initiated to this experience after a severe identity crisis presents a particular problem. After a profound crisis in which one has nearly lost his moorings in life, the onset of tongue-speaking often is experienced as a rescue from an abyss. At times, it appears that one's whole life begins to revolve around this experience, often with a militant defensiveness against any self-examination. Some seriously upset persons have sought to keep their personal and professional heads above water by clinging to tongue-speaking. In my opinion, this is the situation among some clergymen who have been impervious to the counseling of their fellow clergy. Some clergy have seemed to prefer masochistically to split congregations and terminate their own pastorates rather than cooperate with the proposals made by their bishops. Such extreme instances are few, but it should be noted that this may be a sign of emotional instability, and an evidence of how a religious context can be used in the service of one's neurotic or psychotic needs.

In summary, my glossolalia research has included an examination of the phenomenon itself, and a study of the theories about it. I have concluded that it is a learned behavior which often brings a sense of power and well-being. It may also lead to excesses resulting in community disruption. The use of glossolalia determines whether it is constructive or not. I hope that the practice of glossolalia will be conducted in the context of what Micah called true religion: doing justice, loving kindness, and walking humbly with God.

BIBLIOGRAPHY ON GLOSSOLALIA

Christenson, Laurence. *Speaking in Tongues.* Minneapolis: Bethany Fellowship, 1968.

Cutten, George Barton. *Speaking with Tongues: Historically and Psychologically Considered.* New Haven: Yale University Press, 1927.

du Plessis, David J. *The Spirit Bade Me Go.* Dallas: David J. du Plessis, 1961.

Frank, Jerome D. *Persuasion and Healing.* Baltimore: The John Hopkins Press, 1961.

Hilgard, E. *Hypnotic Susceptibility.* New York: Harcourt, Brace & World, 1965.

Hoekema, Anthony A. *What About Tongue-Speaking?* Grand Rapids: Wm. B. Eerdmans Publishing Co., 1966.

Kelsey, Morton T. *Tongue-Speaking. An Experiment in Spiritual Experience.* New York: Doubleday & Co., 1964.

Kildahl, John P. *The Psychology of Speaking in Tongues.* New York: Harper & Row, 1972.

Laffal, Julius, *Pathological and Normal Language.* New York: Atherton Press, 1965.

Piaget, Jean. *The Language and Thought of the Child.* New York: Meridian Books, 1955.

Samarin, W. J. *Tongues of Men and Angels: the Religious Language of Pentecostalism.* New York: Macmillan Company, 1972.

Sherrill, John L. *They Speak with Other Tongues.* New York: McGraw-Hill Book Co., 1964.

Wolberg, L., and Kildahl, J. *The Dynamics of Personality.* New York: Grune & Stratton, 1970.

5

Baptized in Water and in Spirit

Arnold Bittlinger
Professor of Systematic Theology
Schloss Craheim, Germany

5

Baptized in Water and in Spirit

The Background of Christian Initiation

Why does the Christian church baptize? Most people would say: Because Christ told us to do so (Matt. 28: 19-20). Some scholars say that Christ said nothing concerning baptism. They interpret the passage in Matthew as a tradition of the early church. The argument goes like this: The early church needed some kind of initiation, and so it borrowed a rite which was already common among the Jews and to some extent also in Hellenism.

It is not necessary to argue with people who say that certain words in the Bible were not spoken by the historic Christ, but by the early church. The risen and exalted Christ is as real as the historic Christ. If the exalted Christ spoke to his church, it is as much the word of Jesus as when someone wrote down the words of the historic Jesus. In either case we can conclude that the early Christians baptized because Jesus told them to do so.

Baptism, however, was not uniquely a Christian rite. It was common in the world of the New Testament, both in Hellenism (Greek culture), and in Judaism (Jewish culture).

In Hellenism water had a double meaning. It was regarded as death-bringing as well as life-giving. One can understand these meanings when one considers life in the Mediterranean world of Greek culture. Water could destroy people, for instance, in horrible storms (sailing in those times was often dangerous). Yet, water was essential to existence. It gave life to crops and thus to man.

The water of the Nile River was especially looked upon as a divine element. There are ancient Egyptian pictures of a priest pouring a pitcher of water from the Nile River over a corpse. The droplets of water are portrayed in the form of hieroglyphs representing life.

In Judaism there are various ritual washings which are mainly based on the Old Testament. Ritual washings and baptism also played a role in the Qumran Community, from which the Dead Sea Scrolls came. Closest, however, to the Christian concept of baptism is Jewish proselyte baptism. In proselyte baptism, one who wanted to become a Jew was first instructed about the seriousness of the step being taken. If he still wanted to become a Jew, he was circumcised. After the wound of circumcision had healed, he was brought to the baptismal pool. Two or three rabbinic students would stand at his side, as witnesses, and would clarify the commandments. During this time, water was already covering the lower half of his body. If he was still earnest about his decision, he was then ducked under the water so that his entire body was covered. From the moment he stepped out of the baptismal font, he was considered in every respect an Israelite. Children were baptized along with their parents. But they had the right, after they had grown up, to decide for themselves if they wanted to remain Jews or not.

A further type of pre-Christian baptism is that of John the Baptist. John preached a baptism of repentance for the forgiveness of sins (Mark 1:4). Closely connected with John's baptism was the prophecy that Jesus would baptize with the Holy Spirit: "I have baptized you with water; but he will baptize you with the Holy Spirit" (Mark 1:8).

Jesus' own baptism by John involved, besides his being baptized in water, the descent of the Holy Spirit upon him, which in a sense pre-figures Christian baptism, as prophesied by John. In receiving the Holy Spirit, Jesus received the power of God. He is thus equiped to carry out his ministry.

The Greek word for "power" is *exousia;* in the Gospels it is used in the same sense that Paul uses *charismata* ("spiritual gifts").

This *exousia* manifests itself in victory over temptation (Mark 1:13), in the power to call disciples (Mark 1:17), in the power to teach (Mark 1:21f.), in the power over demons (Mark 1:25), in the power to heal (Mark 1:31), and in the power to pray (Mark 1:35). Thus receiving the Holy Spirit is an indication of the ordination of Jesus for his service.

John Calvin, the great systematic theologian of the Reformation, understood Jesus' baptism as having significance not only for his own life and ministry, but also for the church: "All the gifts of the Spirit have their wellspring in the Anointing of the Holy Spirit which Jesus received at His baptism. In His baptism Jesus Christ received the Spirit in order to share Him with us."

A further aspect of Christ's baptism is seen in his death. Jesus spoke of his sufferings and death using the picture of baptism: "I have a baptism to be baptized with; and how I am constrained until it is accomplished!" (Luke 12:50). His suffering was accomplished when he said on the cross: "It is finished" (John 19:30). In both instances, the same Greek word is used. (According to Mark 10:38-39, Christ also received the baptism of suffering to share it with us.)

These four models of baptism were already present before the early church began to baptize—the baptismal rites in Hellenism, the baptismal rites in Judaism, the baptism of John the Baptist, and the event of Jesus' own baptism, including his 'baptism of death'. And with the baptism of Jesus we already have a transition to Christian baptism, pre-figuring important elements in the baptismal practice of the early church.

Christian Baptism in the New Testament

In *Christian baptism* the determining factor is the receiving of the Holy Spirit (repentance and forgiveness of sins were already present in the baptism of John). The promise of John the Baptist, that all shall be baptized with the Spirit, which is mentioned in all four gospels, was fulfilled at Pentecost and since then holds for every Christian baptism. If the baptism is not connected with the receiving of the Holy Spirit, then something very important is missing. John's baptism as well as Christian baptism is only genuine if it is connected with receiving the Spirit

(Acts 8:16-19; 19:2-7). *Therefore, the gift of the Holy Spirit is not just an aspect of baptism, but it is the basic element of Christian baptism. Christian baptism is always a baptism with water and with Spirit.*

According to the accounts of the Acts of the Apostles, the receiving of the Holy Spirit can be recogized by the practicing of charismata. Also in Mark 16:16ff., baptism is connected with the promise of charismata. *Where* the Holy Spirit is present, *there* he wants to become manifest.

Besides repentance, forgiveness of sins, and charismata, we also have the element of *faith* as an aspect of baptism in the early church. In Mark 16:16 we read, "He who has believed and has been baptized will be saved."

In Acts 16:31-33, we see the clear connection between faith and baptism, in the case of the Philippian jailer: " 'Believe in the Lord Jesus, and you will be saved, you and your household.' And they spoke the word of the Lord to him and to all that were in his house. And he took them the same hour of the night, and washed their wounds, and he was baptized at once, with all his family."

Since the Reformation, discussions on baptism have raised the question as to whether or not faith necessarily *precedes* baptism. We quote two extreme views:

Carl Schneider, a Lutheran theologian, writes: "Baptism is purely an act of God in which man is completely passive. It does not make any difference who is baptizing or who is baptized. Here, God alone is acting, through the symbol of water, upon the person who is baptized. The only pre-requisite for baptism is the divine epiphany documented in the preaching of the Word and in the water, but not human faith or will."

On the other hand, Johannes Schneider, a Baptist theologian, writes: "For the early Church it is self-evident that one can be baptized only if one believes and confesses his faith in Jesus. Baptism is an act through which those who believe in Christ are accepted into the community of the disciples of Christ. It is impossible to baptize a person who has no faith."

The mere fact that two respected theologians can express these opposite views, shows that there is no clear text in the New Testament which says that faith must precede baptism. (The only verse that stipulates faith as a pre-requisite for baptism, Acts 8:37, is not found in the earliest manuscripts).

This does not mean that we can have baptism without faith—it is only a question of sequence. What we can say with certainty, is that in the early church faith and baptism belong together.

Thus we have in the early church four aspects which are connected with baptism: repentance, forgiveness, faith, and charismata.

Besides these aspects, Paul denotes baptism as dying and rising with Christ (Rom. 6). This aspect is already prefigured in the baptismal rites of Judaism and Hellenism.

In both Judaism and Hellenism, baptism symbolized the idea of death and rising—the end of an old way of life, the beginning of a new life. Thus when Paul links Christian baptism with Christ's baptism of death, describing it as a dying and rising with Christ (Rom. 6:4), he is using terminology which could be understood both by Jews and Greeks.

The Jews were reminded of their proselyte baptism in which the whole body had to be covered with water.

After having been baptized, the proselyte was looked upon as a completely new person. The old person had died and the new person was born. This was even taken in a quite literal sense, so that a child who was born after his parents had been baptized was considered their firstborn child, even though there may have been other children before. According to some rabbinic teaching, if a person had committed a crime before his baptism, this was not even counted against him, because now he was a completely new person.

The Greeks were reminded of their mystery initiations, which were closely tied with baptism. Before the initiation, the one to be initiated was regarded as one who was about to die. After his initiation, he received new life and participated in the life of the god—so went their belief. It was an identification with the dying and rising god. This belief was symbolized by a new robe which was put on by the one who had been initiated.

Paul uses language similar to the mystery cults when he writes in Galatians 3:27, "As many of you as were baptized, so that Paul can say in Galatians 2:20, "It is no longer I who live, but Christ who lives in me."

This mystical union with Christ has ethical consequences for Paul. One who is united with Christ in this way should also walk in obedience to Christ: "Consider yourselves dead to sin and alive to God in Christ Jesus" (Rom. 6:11); "If then you have been raised with Christ, seek the things that are above . . . for you have died, and your life is hid with Christ in God" (Col. 3:1, 3).

Thus Paul points out two further elements in Christian baptism: *mystical union* with the dying and rising Christ, and walking in the love of Christ.

The Gospel of John introduces the term of *rebirth* in connection with baptism (John 3:1-8). Human, physical birth is not enough. In the first birth we receive biological life; but this life is not able to enter into the kingdom of God. One must be 'born anew'; in this rebirth one receives spiritual, eternal life. This rebirth, by water and Spirit, is the pre-requisite for entrance into the kingdom of God (John 3:5). Indeed, until one is born anew, he cannot even 'see' the kingdom of God (vs. 3): without this divine, eternal life, one cannot even understand the spiritual world.

In summary, New Testament teaching links these seven elements to Christian baptism:

1. Baptism and Repentance
2. Baptism and Forgiveness
3. Baptism and Faith
4. Baptism and Rebirth
5. Baptism and Charismata
6. Baptism and Union with the Dying and Rising Christ
7. Baptism and Walking in the Love of Christ

These seven aspects may be grouped into three main aspects. First, I take together repentance, forgiveness, and faith as the *conversion aspect.* Second, I take together rebirth (receiving the *charisma* of eternal life; Rom. 6:23) and the exercise of *charismata* as the *charismatic aspect.* Third, I take together union with the dying and rising

Christ and walking in the love of Christ as the *union aspect.*

These three main aspects are not only connected with baptism, but they are also symbolized by baptism.

THE CONVERSION ASPECT: When the person being baptized is put under the water, it signifies that he is dying to Satan and sin (repentance). When he rises out of the water, it signifies that his sins are washed away (forgiveness) and that he is now putting his trust in Jesus Christ as his Savior (faith).

THE CHARISMATIC ASPECT: When the person being baptized is put under the water, it signifies that he dies to the old self-life. He rises out of the water as a new man with eternal life (rebirth). He is now yielding to Christ who through the Holy Spirit is now operating through his life (exercise of *charismata*).

THE UNION ASPECT: When the person being baptized is put under the water, it signifies that he is brought into union with the suffering and dying Christ. When he rises out of the water, he is identified with the risen and exalted Christ (union with the dying and rising Christ), who henceforth lives in him and lets his love shine through him (union with the love of Christ).

We have evidence that in the early church these three aspects of baptism were made vivid by added symbolism, some of which is still preserved today, especially in the Eastern Orthodox Church. Besides the baptism itself, the liturgy includes the laying on of hands, anointing with oil, celebration of the Eucharist, spitting on Satan, and the use of other symbols such as salt, light, and a new robe. Such symbols portray the manifold richness of Christian initiation. They help create a vital expectancy, both for the one being baptized, and for the congregation of believers who are witnesses to this event.

Baptism in the New Testament is thus far more than a hollow ritual or ceremony. It is a divinely appointed initiation which includes the aspects of *conversion, charismata* and *union with Christ.*

Baptism and Experience

If we compare the meaning of baptism in the New Testament with the reality of baptized people today, one large question arises: If Christian baptism includes all these aspects, why do we have so many baptized criminals, baptized atheists, baptized lukewarm and self-righteous Christians? In short, why do we have so many baptized people who seem not to be Christians at all? There is only one answer to this question: *What God has given in baptism must be actualized in the life of the individual.*

While baptism is an event which occurs at a particular moment in a person's life, both Catholic and Protestant tradition recognize that the efficacy of baptism is not tied to the moment of time wherein it is administered (cf. Augustine, *Epistola* 187, 6, 21; *Westminster Confession* XXX, 6). What is given in baptism may become active or realized at other moments in the life of the believer.

In baptism one is given everything that he will ever receive in Christ—*potentially.* But if that baptism is not *actualized* in the life of the baptized, God's purpose in baptism has failed of achievement. It would have been better if the person had not been baptized at all. The potential given in baptism must be appropriated in the personal experience of the individual.

Ulrich Valeske, a Lutheran theologian, writes: "Baptism gives the reality, potentiality and possibility, but it cries out for actualization in the life of the Christian." That means, every Christan should encounter in his experience at least in some way the different aspects which are connected with baptism.

He should have at least some kind of conversion experience in which he encounters Jesus Christ as his Savior.

He should also have at least some kind of charismatic experience in which he encounters Jesus Christ as the head of his body which is the church.

Finally, he should have at least some kind of union expeperience in which he encounters Jesus Christ as the center of his life.

Let us look briefly at these three experiences:

The Conversion Experience:

The essence of conversion is that we (a) recognize, renounce, and turn away from our sins, (b) approach Christ in faith, to receive forgiveness. This may be a quiet encounter which takes place in the heart, with little or no outward display or evidence. Calvin's sparing mention of his experience in 1532 seems to indicate that his encounter with Christ was of this nature: "God by a sudden conversion subdued and brought my mind to a teachable frame." On the other hand, the actualization of the conversion aspect may be an experience accompanied by great personal upheaval, and marked by outward signs or behavior. In this regard one thinks of a man like Martin

Luther, who describes his conversion experience with the following words: "My soul was thrilled with a gladness such as I had never known before in all my life." Romans 1:17 became "the gate of Paradise" for him.

Inasmuch as the conversion experience has specifically to do with the question of *sin,* many people have been helped to a genuine and deep experience of conversion through the practice of *confession.* This rings a little strange in Protestant ears, though a number of Protestant groups have rediscovered and reclaimed this practice in more recent years.

Theoretically, you can confess your sins directly to God, and receive forgiveness. And yet there seem to be times and situations where the theory doesn't work out in practice. This appears to have been the experience of the early church, as reflected in the word of Scripture, "Confess your sins to one another" (James 5:16). We sometimes need the help of private confession to spring loose a sin, so we can actually be freed from its power and accusation.

Further, there is a need to be specific about our sins. The general confession that "I am a sinner—all men are sinners" can actually cover up specific sins. We can make such a general confession every Sunday in church. Yet if a neighbor calls to our attention some specific sin, how quick we are to deny it, to defend ourselves.

Private confession also affords the advantage of personal absolution. Having confessed your sins, you hear with your own ears the word of forgiveness, spoken by the person to whom you confess.

God knows the weakness of our human nature. He knows that there are times when we need to receive the assurance of forgiveness in a special and personal way. And so he has given to his church this special authority, "If you forgive the sins of any, they are forgiven" (John 20:23).

Philip Melanchthon, one of the Reformers, wrote: "Private absolution is as necessary as baptism. You may hear the Good News proclaimed to the whole of Christendom. But it does not really touch you until the assurance of forgiveness is spoken to you, personally and specifically. One does not really long for grace, unless he longs to hear the voice of God address him personally. Faith recognizes that the Absolution is the accomplishment of *God's* Word, not merely man's word. The woman who was a sinner (Luke 7:47ff.) knew with absolute certainty that her guilt was utterly taken away when she heard Christ's voice: 'Your sins are forgiven.' That is the same kind of assurance that you should have when a Christian brother declares your sins forgiven."

The Charismatic Experience:

The essence of a charismatic experience is the experience of encountering Jesus Christ as the head of his body, which is the church (Eph. 1:22-23; 1 Cor. 12:27), who gave gifts and ministries to men (Eph. 4:8; 1 Cor. 12:28).

He, first of all, gives the charisma of eternal life (Rom. 6:23). All other charismata have their basis in this charisma. All charismata are connected with the body of Christ (1 Cor. 12:12ff.). If we have union with Christ (the head), we also have union with Christians (the members). According to its very essence, a charismatic experience is an experience of yielding. In a charismatic experience the emphasis is not on an outward phenemenon, but on the fact that we allow Christ and his Spirit to work through us. What *we* say or do is of little importance, but what God performs through us is important. As long as we trust in *our* talents, and in *our* ability to speak and to act, we are in no need of God's gifts and graces (Luke 5:31-32). As long as we are convinced that *we* are able to discern the spirits, we do not need the gift of discernment (1 Cor. 12:10). As long as we are convinced that *we* know how to organize, we do not need the charisma of administration (1 Cor. 12:28). As long as we are strong and *know* how to pray and to intercede, we are in no need of assistance from the Spirit, and we will therefore not have the experience that "the Spirit helps our weakness" and "intercedes for us" and "for the saints according to the will of God" (Rom. 8:26-27). Every Christian can put his trust either in his own strength and knowledge or he can recognize his own poverty and yield to the Lord in the expectation that the Holy Spirit will work through him.

If we trust in our own strength and knowledge, we may be misled in the same tragic way as the scribes and Pharisees (Matt. 9:34; 12:24; 26:66-67; cf. also 23: 13ff.). But if we yield to the Lord, then we will have the experience that he speaks and works through us (1 Peter 4:11) "for the common good" (1 Cor. 12:7). Thus the decisive element in a charisma is not the outward appearance, but its function, that it serves "for edification" (1 Cor. 14:26).

Especially suitable for a charismatic experience, would be the day of our confirmation, or if we have a special ministry in the church, also the day of our ordination (if we are married, also the day of our wedding!). It would be appropriate to underline the meaning of these events by an act of yielding to Christ, in order that he may work through us and thus in a new way.

The Union Experience:

In the union experience, we are not concerned primarily with our sins, or with our words and deeds, but we are longing for union with Christ, in order that he may become the very center of our life. It is an experience of resting in Christ, expressed wonderfully in Gerhard Tersteegen's hymn, translated by John Wesley:

> Thou hidden Love of God,
> Whose height, whose depth
> unfathomed no man knows;
> I see from far thy beauteous light,
> Inly I sigh for thy repose.
> My heart is pained, nor can
> it be at rest,
> Till it finds rest in thee.

Through the union with Christ, we experience God as our loving Father (John 14:6). A union experience may have a large scale of variety. It may reach from a simple encounter with Jesus in a daily, quiet period up to an experience of a total mystical union in a beatific vision. It may be combined with an experience of praying and singing in the Spirit, or with an overwhelming awareness of God's love.

But the important thing about a union experience is neither the intensity nor the peculiarity, but the consciousness of the fact that "I have been crucified with Christ;

it is no longer I who live, but Christ who lives in me" (Gal. 2:20). Especially suitable for an experience of union with Christ is Holy Communion. Here we are joined mystically and really with the dying and rising Christ. We become one with him. In eating the bread and drinking the wine, we experience the fact that Jesus enters our bodies and fills us with himself. The fruit of such a union with Christ is a Christ-like life. Holy Communion is a communion of the New Covenant, wherein the law of God is written on our hearts (Jer. 31:33). As we remain in this union with Christ, our deeds will be full of the love of Christ.

In a normal worship service all three aspects are combined:

1) Confession of sins, receiving absolution, and confession of faith (conversion aspect)

2) Preaching, Bible reading, singing, praying, offering, and mission into the world (charismatic aspect)

3) Holy Communion and silence (union aspect)

Every worship service can thus recreate and reinforce the actualizations which we may have experienced in various ways and at various times.

6

The Congregation and the Gifts

J. Elmo Agrimson

6

The Congregation and the Gifts

When one reads the Pauline Epistles one cannot miss the focus of the writer's concern for the congregation, the body of Christ. As a matter of fact, he considered the inability to discern or identify this body, a kind of heresy. Believers were to be recognized not for their individual bizarre excellence but for their ability to identify with the spirit of Christ in the group. In the eleventh chapter of 1 Corinthians we read beginning with the 28th verse, "Let a man examine himself, and so eat of the bread and drink of the cup. For any one who eats and drinks without discerning the body eats and drinks judgment upon himself." Gifts of the body (the fellowship of Christians), therefore, were intended to assist this group of people in expressing the love of Christ. Any activity of an individual which divided the group was held in question by St. Paul. Making the matter of eating a primary indulgence reflected on the value of what they were doing. If a person relies on a sensational phenomenon like speaking in tongues to show faith, then he is out of focus with the fellowship.

The Work of the Spirit

Without a doubt, St. Paul approved of speaking in tongues, but he warns, "Nevertheless, in church I would rather speak five words with my mind, in order to instruct others, than ten thousand words in a tongue" (1 Cor. 14:19).

The Christian church emerges out of a New Testament, a new covenant, a new age, background. Accompanying this expectation and revealing its quality is the Holy Spirit, the Comforter.

"The New Testament is uniquely a book of the Holy Spirit with every one of its writings except 2 and 3 John containing references to the Spirit. It announces the fulfillment of prophecy, the arrival of the new age of the Spirit which begins with the completion of the work of Jesus. Characteristic of the synoptic Gospels is their presentation of the Spirit as the Messianic endowment of Jesus. . . . Peculiar to the Fourth Gospel is the account of the bestowal of the Spirit upon the disciples by their risen Lord in a manner reminiscent of the divine 'breathing' in Genesis 2:7 (John 20:22). The Acts of the Apostles describes in detail the fulfillment of the promise of the Spirit. His coming amid the ecstasy of Pentecost, interpreted as the vindication of Jesus' Messiahship and the inauguration of the Messianic age, marks the establishment of the church as a historical reality (Acts 2). But the whole history of the apostolic church is a continuation of Pentecost. Not only were there repeated outpourings of the Spirit (Acts 4:31; 8:17; 10:44; 19:6), but the very existence of the new fellowship depended on the guidance, power, and gifts of the Spirit. The emphasis appears to be on the Spirit as an extraordinary and supernatural power manifest in visions, signs and wonders, and bestowing such *charismata* as healing, exorcism, glossolalia, and prophecy. It is clear, however, that the Spirit is also the author and guide of Christian life in general and that there is no genuine Christian life 'on the wrong side of Pentecost.'

"The activities of the Spirit, furthermore, are personal in nature: He speaks, bears witness, appoints for service, forbids, and approves. Paul, the foremost interpreter of the work of the Spirit, recognizes the *charismata,* the extraordinary gifts of the Spirit, but subordinates them to *charis,* the grace which initiates and sustains ordinary Christian life." [1]

Note that the Spirit relates to quality of life rather than to languages spoken (Acts) or tongues expressing ecstasy (1 Cor.). Thus the congregational model of charismatic understanding focuses in 1 Corinthians rather than in Acts.

It is therefore, important for us to remember that the charismatic or pentecostal movement is not intended to be a collection of individual practitioners. The charismatic movement intends to allow for the free activity of the Holy Spirit, cultivation of a quality of warm fellowship and a more personal identity of the body of Christ in our time. We are faced with the same dilemma as St. Paul saw in the church at Corinth. All of us have various degrees of neurotic tendencies, egotistical needs and even sensual appetities that easily flow through subjective vehicles of expression. Safeguards are needed to avoid making sensationalism, feelings approaching hysteria, and group induced excitement, examples of the visitation of the spirit. This can become religious exhibitionism.

Reaction Against Structure

Without a doubt, our time has precipitated a reaction to a rationalistic, formal, controlled, institutional religious style. For this reason the movement tends to be critical of our traditional theological discipline. A pastor writes, "The dominant thrust of our theological seminaries is intellectual and dogmatic. Our pastors are well-versed in theology. They know how to think. And yet people don't think up winds, they feel winds . . . they experience winds. And so it is with the Holy Spirit. The Holy Spirit meets us at the level of experience, of the subjective, and all the intellectual analysis we can muster cannot convince a person that he has not experienced something when he has." [2] He does not mean we should recklessly cast off the traditional experience of the church. Throughout the ages she has been guided by her doctrinal history. This pastor respects the authority of Scripture for guidance and support in the congregations. Other charismatics may narrow the themes of Scripture to the more individualized activity in Acts and 1 Corinthians.

Our society often demonstrates moods of depression and despair which may call forth pessimistic religious outlooks. I have often observed in the charismatic followers that their self-image has been low and self-effacing. Despite claims of being filled with the Spirit, there is constant reference to "I am worthless," "I'm just a dirty rag." A disclaimer on this world's beauty and joy prevails. Hope retreats to a spiritual distance, often the second coming of Jesus. A mood of floating on a cloud of ecstatic feeling gives one the impression that the natural world has been enveloped by gloom, despair, and futility. Such mental attitudes pass by Easter's hope, joy, and creativity.

Religious experiential phenomena demands respect. Everyone is entitled to do his own thing. It is a very serious matter to pass judgment on the validity of another person's religious lifestyle. The problem comes when, like the Corinthians, a pentecostal will imply, if not directly state, that what he experienced must be the experience of another. "The wind blows where it wills" (John 3:8). We cannot always identify where or why it comes.

The Spirit and the Church

The issue constantly comes back to "what is the church?" Gustav Aulen says this well. "The church has been defined as the dominion of Christ and as a fellowship created by the Spirit. The essential nature of the church is thereby indicated. No other definition can supersede this interpretation or come into conflict with it. If we speak of the church as 'the communion of saints,' the significance of this phrase becomes clear only when we note that it does not refer to any subjective holiness which might serve as a starting point for the establishment of the church. The church can be called the communion of saints only because the Holy Spirit here accomplishes his sanctifying work in the world. The phrase, 'a fellowship created by the Spirit,' indicates that which is essential for the Christian church, if we thereby maintain that this Spirit of Jesus Christ, and that the Christian church through this creation by the Spirit is also a creation of the finished and continuous work of Christ." [3]

There is a temptation frequently to imply that we should ask for an extra power from on high even if we already are Christians or have been faithful to our baptismal vow. "Extra power" may be a substitute for faith in Jesus and the invisible spirit moving among us. "Extra power" possibly reveals a cry for identity and support from the Christian group. If the church does not have fellowship support, the individual will cry in a vertical direction.

"As a Luthacostal, let me state that every baptized believer has the Holy Spirit and that the Baptism with the Holy Spirit is not necessary for salvation. However, if God has anything for us then not wanting or not seeking it would be an insult to His grace. . . . If you are a believer and have been baptized then you are clothed with power from on High but you may not yet have experienced or claimed the fullness of the power. You might live all your life as a poor man and then discover on your deathbed that your name was really Rockefeller." [4] When experience becomes a norm or test of the faith the varied possibilities of personality often are hurt for those who do not conform. Again this mood or subjective judgment violates the sanctity of privacy and natural expression.

I think we can expect that our time will have many religious moods blowing through our churches. These will be less committed to traditional theological guidelines and thorough scriptural exegesis. Scriptural references will emphasize isolated themes and verses. The movement thus easily moves across denominational lines—Catholic, Lutheran, Episcopalian. To compensate for the alienation and loneliness of our time we can expect an intensity of religious expression to compensate for futility, loss of control of physical environment, social guilt over war, pollution, racism, fear of technology and dehumanization. Nostalgia—a longing for a more simple, intimate, dependent, and authoritative, alleged good old time—clouds the atmosphere. Such crises of the human spirit have often precipitated ghost dances and expectation of messianic delivery from powerlessness.

Why does the charismatic phenomenon often create dissension and polarization in congregations? How shall we deal with it? We must begin with the acceptance of the various kinds of expressions of the faith. I have found no better guideline than 1 Corinthians, Chapters 11-14: here is a case study; a theological description of the church; a practical answer; the greatest gift is *love!* The Holy Spirit allows freedom for various styles for the individual and the group to say how their experience with Jesus has affected them.

A frequent source of tension in the church visited by the charismatic phenomenon, comes from describing the second blessing or baptism of the Holy Spirit. This point needs careful thinking. "God does not simply want that we should have an experience of the presence of his Spirit; he also wants us to experience the Spirit's transforming power. This is the element of truth in the insistence which some Christian groups place on the Second Blessing or the Baptism of the Spirit. They usually err, however, by indicating earthly, psychological criteria by means of which to recognize that the event has taken place, forgetting that, just as it is possible for many people to be born again without a violent or sudden experience of conversion, so the power of the Spirit may manifest itself in an individual's life without definite outward signs. The power of the Spirit can be measured only by the fruit we bear, that is, by the spiritual life we engender in other people; and that is a fact not so easily noticeable and often completely hid from us. There are people whose life is a great spiritual blessing for many, yet they are hardly aware of it." [5]

Testing the Spirits

We need more informal opportunity for talking about the faith in our congregations. More intervals or moments of mystic reflection could cultivate wholesome qualities of intimacy in the church. At the same time it is imperative that we have a focus of theological reference to keep our moods from carrying us along with a religious expression without regard for the community of believers, without concern for social responsibility, without courageous efforts for justice. Love still must be *the* criteria for defining the Christian. The Christian thereby brings a bit of heaven to this earth. To affirm creation and assume responsibility for a complex and fast changing technological age demands great gifts of hope and mental concentration. It is not intended that the Christian should escape on a cloud awaiting the end of the world. We shall look for a new heaven and a new earth among us now. This kind of world view includes the intimacy and warmth of the fellowship of the body of Christ.

To be disciples of Jesus means that we have our feet on the ground, our face turned to new days, our expressions of love let loose to assist one another. The church has a rich heritage of theological tradition to assist us and guide us. The two dangers I most often see are the individualized authority that ignores the "testing of the spirits" by the group and the receding from the meaning of creation including the value of being human in Christ, the new creation. A religious movement without sound theological moorings will become a children's crusade. The flamboyant emotions of religious ecstasy will toss the participants on the rocks and tumults of human ambitions and conflict.

"The variety of theological traditions is a thing to be treasured. No one tradition has managed to exploit to the full the richness of God's gift in Jesus Christ and his Holy Spirit. Further I would recommend that a charismatic theologian will make his greatest contribution by working out the theology of the Pentecostal experience with the categories of his own denominational tradition. . . . But if the Lutheran Neo-Pentecostal is to be of service to those who need a theology of the Pentecostal spirituality within a Lutheran framework it will not do to take over uncritically the Wesleyan or the Pentecostal categories. The Lutheran Neo-Pentecostals must set the Pentecostal spirituality within the authentic Lutheran Theological tradition." [6]

Summary and Observations

1. Charismatic emphasis prevails in many congregations and major denominations in America. It should be recognized as a sincere, devout participation of many church members.

2. The charismatics deserve respect and open acceptance by fellow Christians including those not claiming the same mode of witnessing to the faith.

3. The New Testament describes the church as a body, a community of believers. Gifts—speaking in tongues, prophecy, administration, healing—are not to be individual attention attracters (like sparklers at a Fourth of July celebration). The gifts are to be beneficial to the group, build up the wholesome experience of the spirit of Christ in the church (group). If the gifts become disruptive or troublesome to the group they should be suspended, evaluated, or redirected (1 Cor. 12). "Nevertheless, in church I would rather speak five words with my mind, in order to instruct others, than ten thousand words in a tongue" (1 Cor. 14:19).

4. One baptism—water and the word—constitutes the Christian baptism. Baptism of the Holy Spirit begins with infant baptism. Moments of new insight or joyous feeling may occur at several points later in life. These should not be called another baptism, but a new awareness of the life in Christ. This includes a sensitive perception of my neighbor and creation.

5. Charismatic people with gifts, which should really include all Christians, need the theological framework over which the body of Christ is developed. It is only with this kind of framework that the church can function, pulsate, and radiate its qualities of love, courage, and hope to her members and to the world around her. Theology, the commitment and the response to the Scriptures with reflective discernment becomes imperative for each generation in the church. We need such tools to sort out the many

moods and varied religious fads. The confessions (doctrinal statements) of the church were the lighthouses for dramatic crisis moments in the church. The Christian today needs the clear bell and directional beacon of both mind and feeling.

6. Charismatic gifts have their best meaning in the continuity of the tradition (doctrine, liturgy, and history) of the church. Disruptive, fighting, and fragmented Christian groups can not boast of the gifts of the Spirit. Paul addresses himself very strongly to this predicament in the Corinthian church. The church in Corinth is an excellent point of reference for any group that is deliberating over how to understand the gifts of the church.

7. The charismatic movement needs the balance of creation theology. The explanation to the First Article of the Creed (Luther's Catechism) calls us to be stewards, creators, neighbors. Here we express our gifts. This is the stage or global chancel where we sing our praise to God the Creator.

8. The charismatics can develop into a kind of Jesus cult, a mystical other-worldly monastic attitude. Jesus said, "As thou didst send me into the world, so I have sent them into the world." In Christ God was lighting the darkness of the world, not escaping it.

9. Charismatics should demonstrate social concern. Awareness of the neighbor reveals the chief need for gifts. Sensitivity and love become the major effect of the gifts in 1 Corinthians 13.

10. In this time of estrangement, aloneness, and uprooting of familiar social patterns, the church must have

a sensitive awareness of the Spirit's moving among us, not only to declare the mystery of God but the mystery and wonder of our fellow human beings, that we are to be in touch with each other through Jesus Christ. The Incarnation calls us to be the new humanity with joy in being human because his Spirit is among us.

Notes

1. T. A. Kantonen, "Holy Spirit" in *The Encyclopedia of the Lutheran Church* (Minneapolis: Augsburg Publishing House, 1965), II, pp. 1037-1038.
2. Bernhard W. Lien, "The Pastor: Windbreak or Windmill."
3. Gustav Aulen, *The Faith of the Christian Church,* (Philadelphia: Fortress Press, 1961), p. 354.
4. Erwin E. Prange, "What's Happening in Lutheran Spiritual Renewal," an address delivered to the Lutheran Council in the U.S.A., American Missions Planning Consultations, Regions 3 and 4, March 16, 1972, Washington, D.C.
5. Otto A. Piper, "The Power of the Christian Life," *Theology Today,* January, 1955.
6. Kilian McDonnell O.S.B., "Baptism in the Holy Spirit as an Ecumenical Problem."